People Are Saying . . .

Dr. Susan's Girls-Only Weight Loss Guide will be a best friend to girls who strive for healthier bodies and happier hearts. Written in an easy-to-read, fun way, the whole family may find themselves passing this book around to read Bartell's—and her teenage advisory panel's—advice on a typical teenager's everyday struggles to maintain a healthy weight and break unhealthy eating patterns.

— D⟨
Se⟨

This book is en⟨   ⟩th stress,
family pressures⟨   ⟩tic goals,
and improving⟨   ⟩er." The
knowledge she h⟨   ⟩irls!

— Sh⟨
Ex⟨

Finally! A book⟨   ⟩ understand and relate⟨   ⟩ to help
them understan⟨   ⟩e themselves. *Dr. Susai⟨   ⟩ to help
empower young⟨   ⟩r works
with a teenage g⟨

— Jei⟨
Sch⟨

For girls who ar⟨   ⟩essages,
Dr. Bartell's boo⟨   ⟩helping
girls understand⟨   ⟩havior
and self-esteem⟨   ⟩. She
also dares to tak⟨   ⟩heir
daughters . . . it's⟨

— Liz⟨
Mar⟨
Autl⟨   ⟩rging

Losing weight is⟨   ⟩feel and
think the same way . . . other books have ha⟨   ⟩emphasize, and Dr. Susan writes so clearly, that moms need to model a healthy lifestyle and teach their daughters to love their own bodies. She inspires the reader to take responsibility for how she looks and feels, and to take the knowledge from this book to take control of becoming what she wants to be!

— **Nancy Lenhart**
Executive Director, Camp La Jolla

Dr. Bartell's book is the first I've seen that deals with the connection between feelings, overeating, and overweight in childhood. She is right on point. Her book contains excellent tips for improving self-love and for coping with emotions without resorting to food. I applaud Dr. Bartell's keen insight and sensitive, practical approach.

— **Robert Pretlow, MD, FAAP**
Director, WeighCool—Overweight in Childhood Internet Intervention Program

Dr. Bartell provides a comprehensive, smart guide for whole living. Every girl and her mother should read *Dr. Susan's Girls-Only Weight Loss Guide* to better understand the relationship between food, and emotional needs and behaviors. It demystifies how we feel about our bodies and our relationship with food.

— **Linda Silva, MS, LMHC**
Editor-in-Chief, *The Parent Guide*

Teens will appreciate the honest talk of Dr. Susan and her teen advisors. If weight is an issue in your life, give yourself this book. Parents concerned for their teens' well-being cannot be better served! Dr. Susan's obvious working knowledge and practical advice provides your teen with the tools to take action.

— **Tut Gramling**
Director, Camp Endeavor

Of the many books written on weight management, *Dr. Susan's Girls-Only Weight Loss Guide* stands out as particularly refreshing. It gives hope and inspiration to the thousands of girls struggling with weight, body image disturbance and poor self-esteem. The factual information provided is based on a solid knowledge of adolescent nutrition, growth and development. Every adolescent girl should read it!

— **Neville H. Golden, M.D.**
Director, Eating Disorders Center, Schneider Children's Hospital, NY

Dr. Bartell offers preteens and teens a masterful approach to taking control of their health, weight, body image and lives. Combining wit, research and wisdom, she helps empower readers to make realistic and wise lifestyle choices—all aimed at promoting total well-being. The moving stories and personal tips of real people sharing their struggles, and offering practical solutions, makes this a unique, must-read book!

— **Judy E. Marshel, PhD, RD, CDN**
Nutritionist specializing in treating eating disorders

Dr. Susan's Girls-Only Weight Loss Guide is a practical, useful guide leading to true success in lifestyle. It brings knowledge to a level of understanding that is necessary to make healthy, effective change in their day-to-day life and empowers young girls to choose wisely!

— **Jean Huelsing**
Director, Camp Jump Start

Dr. Susan's Girls-Only

Weight Loss Guide

The EASY, FUN way to look and feel good!

Dr. Susan's Girls-Only Weight Loss Guide

The EASY, FUN way to look and feel good!

DR. SUSAN S. BARTELL

Parent Positive Press
New York

Publisher's note: The information and advice in this book should not be used instead of medical advice. You should speak to your doctor about your health, especially about things that may need diagnosis or medical attention.

For bulk or special sales please call
(877) 885-BOOK (2665) or email info@parentpositive.com

Published by
Parent Positive Press
446 Willis Avenue #118
Williston Park, NY 11596
http://www.girlsonlyweightloss.com/

ISBN 0–9721502–0–X

Cover design by George Foster
Interior design by Desktop Miracles
Indexing by Wendy Allex

Publishers Cataloging-in-Publication Data

Bartell, Susan S.
    Dr. Susan's girls-only weight loss guide : the easy fun way to look and feel good! / Susan S. Bartell.
        p.   cm.
    Includes index.
    SUMMARY: The book addresses weight loss for teenage girls, including the emotional, nutritional and exercise issues related to losing weight successfully.
    ISBN 0–9721502–0–X
    1. Obesity in adolescence—Juvenile literature.   2. Reducing diets—Juvenile literature.   3. Teenage girls—Nutrition—Juvenile literature.
4. Weight loss.   I. Title.   II. Title: Girls-only weight loss guide.
RJ399.C6B37   2006   613.2'5'0835'2
                                                     QBI05-600161

For the two most important girls in my life

Gillian Emma—who nourishes me with compassion and caring

Mollie Kate—who inspires me with energy and creativity

And for the two most important women in my life

*My mother—for teaching me to stand up for what
I believe in and because we made it through my
teen years to become the best of friends*

*My mother-in-law—for unending support and because
she wishes she'd had this book when she was a teen*

Foreword

You have begun to read *Dr. Susan's Girls-Only Weight Loss Guide*, which means that you are either a teenage girl who is tired and frustrated that you are overweight, or you are an adult who wants to help a teenage girl in your life to lose weight and become healthier. Congratulations! By beginning to read this book, you are taking the first steps toward achieving your goal.

As you may know, there is an epidemic of overweight people in the United States as well as in other westernized countries. This epidemic includes teenage girls. In fact, studies have shown that at least 15 percent of teens are overweight and just as many are at risk for becoming overweight. Overweight teens suffer with high blood pressure, high cholesterol, and even type-two diabetes. But why are so many girls overweight? There are many reasons: including busy lives filled with fast food; genes that a teen inherits from a parent; too much TV or computer time and not enough exercise; money available to spend on food; and eating as a way to cope with feelings.

With all these hurdles to being healthy, what is a girl (or a parent) to do about it? If you are an overweight teenager, you may be asking yourself this question every day. You may have tried diets that have failed, or made resolutions that you haven't been able to keep. Perhaps your parents nag you about eating and exercise. But none of it works. If you are an adult, you are probably worried about your teenager, upset with constant stress and fighting about her weight, and at your wit's end about how to help her.

In my medical practice, over the course of my years as a specialist in adolescent medicine, I have seen many overweight girls suffer with poor self-esteem, social problems, depression, and family stress because they have not yet found a way to help themselves lose weight and become healthier. But, clearly, dieting is not the answer. Teenagers should not deprive their bodies of necessary nutrients in order to lose weight. Also, it is almost impossible to stick to a strict diet that deprives you of foods that you love to eat. Many teenage girls don't know where to turn because they find it embarrassing to even discuss their weight with adults—including parents and even doctors!

As an overweight teenage girl it is very important for your physical and emotional health that you help yourself become healthier. And because you are old enough to start making many choices in your life, this must be your decision, not that of your parents. If you are an adult, it is essential to your role in the life of your adolescent that you encourage her to take responsibility for making important changes in her life—doing it herself and becoming responsible for her own health and happiness.

As a girl reading this book, *Dr. Susan's Girls-Only Weight Loss Guide* offers you a great opportunity to take charge of your health, your body, and your life. You will be able to make changes that are good for you. This is not a fad diet. Rather it is a plan that you can follow as slowly or as quickly as you would like. It will teach you how to help yourself become happier and to achieve a healthy weight loss without developing an eating disorder. This book is for girls only. This is because many eating, social, and family issues are very different for boys and girls. As you read you will find many examples of girls who have had experiences very similar to yours. This will help you stay motivated to become healthier.

As an adult giving this book to a girl you care about, *Dr. Susan's Girls-Only Weight Loss Guide* gives you the chance to help her in a way that doesn't make her feel that you are being intrusive or insulting. This book bridges the gap that until now has been filled with arguments and fights. You can feel confident that you are giving her an effective, practical, and *safe* tool to help herself feel better and become healthier.

As you begin reading, you begin your journey toward a healthier life. Take the first step now and before you know it you will be there.

ANGELA DIAZ, MD, MPH
Director, Mount Sinai Adolescent Health Center,
    Mount Sinai Medical Center;
Professor of Pediatrics, Mount Sinai School of Medicine
New York
August 1, 2005

Acknowledgments

Writing this book has been a dream of mine for many years and seeing it come true has been an incredible experience. However, like most dreams, it only happened because I had a great deal of help and support. Many people gave me their time, knowledge, enthusiasm, and love. They asked for nothing in return and I consider myself blessed to have found each one of these individuals.

I am truly thankful to my Girls Advisory Group, twelve girls who volunteered their time, provided excellent advice and feedback, were awesome editors, and really supported me from beginning to end. They are Alexis Bevilacqua, Montserrat Del Olmo, Chantal Dumpson, Jessica Dumpson, Eve Anne Eichenholtz, Anna Evans, Jaime Feather, Michelle Guidice, Katherine J. Hartman, Michal Lucas, Burgandy-Leigh McCurty, and Kelly Blake Woolf. I also want to thank their parents for allowing and facilitating the participation of their wonderful daughters.

I was also fortunate to have found several people who gave their time and expertise in order to give this book validity and authority. I am very grateful to, Jamie Bliss, Bev Francis, Bonnie Goldstein, Dr. Reed Mangels, Dr. Judy Marshel, Ivy Woolf Turk and Dr. Ira Sacker.

I want to give a huge shout-out to the girls and women of Surprise Lake Camp, summer 2005, for their awesome input and enthusiastic support of this project.

Friendships with women are one of the most important parts of my life, and I value each and every one of them. Two women in particular have provided enormous and unending support of this project for which I am very, very thankful and deeply moved. They are Julie Levi and Jennifer Biblowitz and I love them both very much.

I am supremely lucky to have three amazing children whose support means more to me than I can say. Max, Gillian, and Mollie, I love you to the moon, to the stars, to Brooklyn, and back again.

And, as always, Lew, you are my never-ending love, I would never have been able to begin or complete this book without you.

SUSAN S. BARTELL, PSY.D
September 2005

For Parents and Other Adults

T here is no doubt that *Dr. Susan's Girls-Only Weight Loss Guide* will help girls lose weight or fat and become healthier and feel better about their bodies. In creating this book I believed that the voice of girls would be vital to the book's ability to reach into the heart and soul of a reader. Therefore, I established an advisory group— twelve preteen and teenage girls who read every word and infused the chapters with their own real-life experiences. This advisory group felt strongly that they needed to reach out to adults to help them give this book to their girls. This is such a sensitive subject that in order for the book to be received successfully, an adult needs to give it in a way that would make it likely to be accepted—without a fight or a feeling of rejection (by parent or child). My advisory group therefore offers the adults some helpful suggestions. I'm sure that all girls reading this book will agree with their advice. Below are their words to you.

A Note from the Girls Advisory Group

We spent a lot of time helping to write *Dr. Susan's Girls-Only Weight Loss Guide* and we learned a lot too, so we really want to make sure that many girls get to use all the great ideas and information.

We know that you really want to help your daughter or the girl you care about find a healthy way of living. We also know (because we're teenagers) that when it comes to weight loss, you might be finding it difficult to figure out how to help. Some of us have had a hard time talking to our parents about these things because we end up fighting with them—this happens all over. We feel that sometimes parents and others who are close to a girl want to help so much that they push too hard. This can turn a girl off to what you are saying, so she won't be able to benefit from your help.

We asked Dr. Susan if we could write this note to parents and other adults to give you some suggestions for how to give this book to a girl in a way that will make her want to read it (rather than throwing it at you or feeling really hurt). We also want to give parents some tips for how to help a girl feel better about her body. Dr. Susan thought this was a great idea, so here are our tips:

1. Do give *Dr. Susan's Girls-Only Weight Loss Guide* to the girl you want to help!

2. Don't force her to read it. If you push, it could backfire. She might even refuse to consider that the information in the book will help her. Tell her that you'd be happy to discuss the book, or help her with any part of it (for example, by getting or cooking food that she needs), but don't ask repeatedly if she's read it yet.

3. Be supportive. If she asks for your help with food, exercising or anything else, don't be critical or judgmental. Give her the help she asks for, and tell her you're really proud of her. But don't push her to do more than she's ready for, even if you think she should do it.

4. Let her come to you for help. If you ask too often what changes she's making, you and your daughter (or friend, student, niece or granddaughter) could end up having huge fights. It's okay to offer your help once in a while, but if you do it too often, she'll think you're watching everything she does. This will make her feel that you only care about whether she is changing and not about who she is now.

5. Don't be critical of her or her body. When you give *Dr. Susan's Girls-Only Weight Loss Guide* to her, explain that it is a "life tool." She can use whichever parts *she* thinks will be most helpful. It is important to create an understanding that even though it may be the right time for her to work on having a healthier body or life-style, you don't think there is anything wrong with the person that she is. *Dr. Susan's Girls-Only Weight Loss Guide* is not a solution to every problem and it won't make her become a different person. But it will help her gain control over her life and feel healthier and happier.

6. Learn to understand her and what she feels about herself. She may have great self-esteem even if she is struggling with weight. Or she may feel sad, angry, or even dislike herself. Once you understand how she feels about herself, you will know whether giving her *Dr. Susan's Girls-Only Weight Loss Guide* is enough, or whether she needs more help, like counseling, a nutritionist or even a medical doctor who specializes in weight loss or eating disorders.

7. Model a healthy lifestyle. Don't be critical of your own body in front of any girl because it will teach her to be critical of her own. For example, *don't*:

   * stand in front of the mirror and say "I look fat" or "I hate my thighs/stomach/butt"
   * weigh yourself all the time
   * live on salads
   * exercise constantly

8. **Tell the girl in your life that she is amazing and you love her unconditionally.** Giving her *Dr. Susan's Girls-Only Weight Loss Guide* isn't enough. She also needs kind words, true love, and support to help her feel good about herself.

9. **Read *Dr. Susan's Girls-Only Weight Loss Guide* yourself.** This book teaches a girl about herself as well as other factors that impact her life. It discusses puberty, genetics, family eating patterns, and relationships, some of which you may not have discussed with your daughter or the girls you care about. She may seek you out for help and information, so if you've read the book, it will help the two of you to communicate about these things. Additionally, Dr. Susan told us that adult women often have the same struggles that girls have with weight and body image. So, maybe you'll benefit from the book too.

We know that *Dr. Susan's Girls-Only Weight Loss Guide* will really help girls become healthier and feel happier. Good luck and enjoy the book!

Alexis   Anna   Burgandy

chantal   Eve   Jaime

Jessica   Katherine   Kelly

Michal   michelle   Montserrat

Table of Contents

Been There, Done That!

Separating Feelings from Food

Iknow exactly how you feel. You really hate how you look and you're staring at yourself in the mirror saying you'd like to change your body or change your feelings about your body. You're praying for the willpower to do it and you don't have a clue where to start. Or maybe, your mom gave you this book because she's fed up with arguing about food, your weight or exercise. Maybe you're furious and hurt that she won't just accept you for who you are. But deep down you know that she wants you to be happy, and she can't figure out how to help you. I've been there, right where you are now. I've stood in front of that mirror. And I've cried.

When I was fifteen years old, I gave up competitive figure skating. I decided that spending hours in a cold skating rink wasn't nearly as much fun as hanging out with my friends. It was a great decision, really, because I wasn't that talented at skating. And besides, it freed up a lot of time to concentrate on schoolwork (hang out with my friends), work part-time (check out the great-looking stock boy), and pick up a new hobby (eating!). That's right, when I stopped skating, a lot of my down-time became focused on activities that centered around food (watching soap operas and socializing). What's more, I didn't replace skating with any other exercise, unless you'd call walking around the mall and munching on caramel popcorn exercise. Since I had skated about fifteen hours a week and was now down to about . . . let's call it zero hours, I bet you can imagine what happened. I began to gain weight! No shock there, right? Except that while I was going through it I didn't even realize it was happening.

You see, when you gain a pound at a time you can tell yourself that it's not happening, or that it's temporary, or pretend that it doesn't bother you. But the truth was that by the time I was sixteen I hated the way I looked, especially when I compared myself to my friends. And there was also no denying the fact that guys weren't interested in me.

I pretended that I didn't care, or that I wasn't "ready" to date yet. But I'll admit to you now that I spent many nights crying myself to sleep. To make matters worse, my mom couldn't take it. She spoke to me often about losing weight and eating differently. Now, as an adult and also a mom myself, I realize she was trying her best to help me be happy, but at the time it didn't seem like it. I was always conscious about what I ate and how much, especially in front of my mom and my friends. I was sure that they were watching everything I ate. I began to eat secretly once in a while to avoid that guilty feeling that I always had when I ate in public. Of course, that just made me feel even more guilty—especially when I overate junk food by myself in my room. Another thing that really got to me was when my mom would try and help me find clothes that "flattered my figure." There weren't any! Of course, some things looked better on me than others, but since I wasn't happy with my body, I didn't feel good in clothes, and my mom and I would end up having huge, blow-out fights. She tried to support me, but since I knew she wasn't really happy with my weight, I wasn't inter-ested in her support. I also wasn't thrilled with the constant reminder that I didn't like myself!

When I went to college, it got even worse because there was so much food in the dorms and the cafeteria. I'd always heard that you gain weight in college. Now I knew why! What's more, as I continued to gain weight, I gave up even more control over my eating because it all seemed so hopeless. That meant that I ate even more food, more often, without even trying to eat healthily. But somewhere, in my third year of college, when I was about twenty, a good friend gave me a surprising response to my usual complaints about dieting and hating my body. She suggested that I'd never be able to lose weight or even feel comfortable with my body, if I didn't first feel good about myself. I had always thought it was the opposite—that if I were happy with my body, I'd like myself better. Besides, even if she was right, it wouldn't be easy to do because I'd been feeling bad about myself for so long. So, I must admit that for about a year I ignored what my friend had said.

But at some point during my senior year I began to think about it again. My life was full and, in many ways, satisfying—I had friends, I was doing okay in school, and I was looking forward to working on my career. I remember looking at myself in the mirror one day, and saying, "I am doing fine, so why do I keep eating and why do I let myself look like this?" And standing right there in my dorm room, I had a crazy revelation: Although I had started gaining weight when I stopped skating, I'd *continued* to gain because I used the taste of food to make me feel good whenever I felt down and to feel even better when I already felt good. But, unfortunately, if, like me, you eat every time you have a strong (positive or negative) feeling, you're bound to gain weight. In fact, all along, I was trading a lifetime of liking my body and myself, for a few moments of happiness in tasting the food. My friend had been right all along—if I felt good about myself, or at least dealt with my emotions better, I wouldn't need to eat all the time.

I started to write a food and feelings journal—noting all the food I ate and how I felt when I ate it. It became obvious to me that I ate for many reasons that had nothing to do with hunger, such as sadness, excitement, anger, and anxiety. Writing this journal not only helped me become aware of this, but helped me to stop doing it. Making this change wasn't nearly as difficult as I thought it would be (when you get to Chapter 4, I'll teach you how to do it, too). As I began to pay attention to my feelings, rather than just eating them away, I was able to deal with them better. For instance, if a friend upset me, I'd discuss it with her, rather than eat a box of cookies. The more in control I felt, the more I liked myself—wow, that was amazing!

As I started to feel better about myself as well as stronger and more determined, I decided to work on improving my body. I began to pay attention to my eating and exercise habits and I began to feel a strong desire to feel good about my body. Sometimes it was a bit difficult because making healthy choices isn't always easy. At other times it was simple—but either way, it was definitely worth it. When I became healthy, I realized that in order to maintain it, I'd have to keep working at it. Now as an adult, I still work at it—eating in a healthy way, exercising, all of it! Oh, and in case you're wondering, my mom and I are now best friends.

Looking back on my teen years, I realize that if I'd had the knowledge and tools, I could've started even sooner on the track to feeling good about my body and making choices that would have made me not only healthier, but happier. In fact, in some ways it was just a lucky accident that my friend made me think about it and that I had that incredible revelation connecting eating and feelings. What if I hadn't made that connection? I might still be miserable today.

Then, when I became a psychologist, I started working with lots of girls and young women. I found out that many have exactly the same worries about their bodies and their weight that I had. I also found out that many had the same reasons for eating that I had—to stuff down feelings. I also found out that girls overeat for other reasons too. For example, some of these girls come from families that overeat, eat poorly, or don't exercise. Others gain weight because they go on and off diets, and still others are overweight because they have inherited the genes for weight gain from someone in their family—just like eye or hair color. By teaching girls how to separate feelings from food and showing them how to break unhealthy patterns and understand their bodies better, I have been able to help many girls become healthier and happier. And as I helped these girls I began to realize that there are many more girls out there who I wanted to reach and help. I wanted to give them the hope, encouragement, and the skills they need to find motivation and inner strength to handle the pressures they are feeling from all sides: family, friends, the media, the fashion world, and the food industry. *That's why I've written this book*—to show you the way to a healthier, happier you! I know the problems, from personal experience and from years of professional training and work with hundreds of girls. I also know the solutions—the very ones I'm giving you in the following pages. In *Dr. Susan's Girls-Only Weight Loss Guide*, I will talk about all these things and many more. I will help you address all the issues that concern you so that you, too, can begin on the journey to becoming healthier and happier.

You have my word—this book is for you. Throughout the chapters, you'll see many examples of girls who have had exactly the same struggles as you. What's more, I've discussed every page of it with girls ranging in age from twelve to nineteen. In fact, to ensure that this book will really help girls, I formed a **Girls Advisory Group**. It was made up of twelve awesome, amazing girls from 12 to 18 years old, representing a range of ethnic groups, shapes, and sizes (you can see their names on the Acknowledgments page, and at the end of the book they share their feelings and thoughts). They've read and critiqued every word I wrote. They were tough on me, but they are also a part of the reason you will love this book—they poured their hearts into it in order to help other girls feel better and live healthier.

The issues, feelings, pressures, and problems will be familiar to you. You will hear from many girls just like yourself, battling with the same things with which you struggle every day. The suggestions and solutions will work with your lifestyle, and are designed especially for girls. You have a right to feel good about your body and yourself. You also have a right to information and knowledge that will give you the *power* to make intelligent changes so you can become healthier and feel happier with your body. Most importantly, you deserve the right to have *control in your own life*. But control comes from making smart, educated choices—that's *real power*. You've come to the right place to help you figure out how to make these things happen healthily and successfully! So start now—begin to read. You can start at the beginning of the book, but if you'd rather jump to the part about exercise, or the part about eating, or the part about families, go right ahead. Just take your first step—it can be a big step or a tiny step. You can read a page or a chapter. As long as you do something to help yourself, you will start to *FEEL* better! Let's begin.

I Don't Like My Body ... but How Do I Take Control and Change It?

A Jealous Secret

Outside it was cold and rainy, but in my office, Kate, Maggie, Lynn, Debbie, and I were deep in conversation about the stress that comes from not liking your body. Kate told her story first:

> "I remember last summer, getting ready for a pool party. I stared at myself in the mirror, hating everything. My thighs rubbed together and no matter how many sit-ups I did, my stomach hung over the top of my shorts. All I could think was 'There is no way I'll ever put on a bathing suit.' I'm embarrassed to admit it, but I didn't even go to the party."

When Kate was finished, Maggie nodded in agreement. "I know just what you mean," she said. "Last week I went shopping with my best friend, Samantha. Everything Sam tried on looked awesome on her. But

I looked awful in all the clothes I tried. In fact, I wouldn't come out of the changing room in any of the outfits. I didn't want to admit to Sam that I needed larger sizes than was available in most of the stores we went into."

This was not the first time I'd heard these girls discussing the feelings that go along with being overweight. In fact, many girls tell me it's a constant struggle to feel good about their bodies and become healthier. To make matters worse, some overweight girls have thin or average-weight friends, mothers, and sisters. These girls tell me that they are secretly jealous, wishing they looked like these girls or women (I remember feeling this when I was a teenager). In fact, some overweight girls purposely choose friends who are also overweight because it makes them feel more comfortable and less jealous. Other girls are able to separate their feelings about friends and family from the way they think about their bodies. But no matter how you deal with your feelings about your body, the majority of overweight girls secretly wish that they looked and felt healthier and slimmer.

This probably all sounds familiar to you, and you're not alone. So now is the time to start thinking about making changes in your life that will make your feel better about yourself. Maybe you're tired of fighting with your mom about your weight or eating habits. Perhaps, like Maggie, you want to feel good about going to the mall with a friend or maybe (the most important reason) you've come to realize that your body is not as healthy as it could be.

How Do I Know I Need to Lose Weight?

If you are not at a healthy weight you're right to want to do something about it. But how do you know for sure that you need to lose weight? Some girls have a poor body image—they *think* they need to lose weight, when their shape, weight, and body size are actually healthy.

You may have heard the term "body image" and wondered what it means. *Your body image is the way you think about your own body and how accurately you see your body for what it really looks like.* If a girl is happy with her body and other people (including her doctor) tell her that her body is at a healthy size, then she has an accurate body image.

But, if a girl is unhappy with her body, even though everyone (especially her doctor) assures her that she looks fine, this means she has a poor body image. If this sounds like you, skip to Chapter 12 and read about eating disorders. Then speak about your feelings to an adult you trust. Losing weight means becoming healthier and looking better, but it does not mean that you should strive to become super skinny—this can be just as unhealthy as being overweight.

On the other hand, a girl *does not have a bad body* image if she is unhappy with her body because she really does need to lose weight (for example, because the doctor told her she should, or because compared to other girls she really does wear a much larger size). If you are unhappy with your body because you realize that if you were healthier then you would feel better, then this book will help you with these things so you can feel better about your body.

Some overweight girls feel content with their bodies. This is a tricky situation because although it is important to have a good body image, it is not good to convince yourself that your body is fine, when actually you aren't as healthy as you could be. Perhaps you don't want to face your real feelings or maybe you are afraid you may not succeed if you do try to lose weight. It's also possible that you do not have an accurate body image—you see yourself as thinner or healthier than you really are. We will discuss these feelings later in the book.

Finding a Healthy Weight for Your Body

You can know for sure whether you need to lose weight (or fat) by taking into account four important factors: your age, height, build, *and* frame. If you weigh more than average for someone of your age, height, build, and frame (all of these!), it may mean that you have more fat on your body than is healthy. But many girls (and even doctors) account for only one or some of these factors when figuring out a desirable, healthy body weight.

For example, 15-year-old Taylor's doctor told her that according to the growth chart she weighed more than she should for her height and age. Taylor was devastated.

"I'm a runner and I'm on the varsity lacrosse team." she told me "I think I eat really well. Once in a while I'll have pizza or ice-cream, but I can't understand how this happened!"

Actually, instead of relying on charts, Taylor's doctor should have looked at *her*. Because she is very athletic, she is more muscular than an average fifteen-year old. Muscle actually weighs more than fat, something that a growth chart does not take into account. Therefore, it did not provide an accurate assessment of Taylor's unusually muscular build. In fact, she has little fat on her body and is extremely healthy. So, although on the chart her weight seems high, in reality her weight is just right for her athletic build.

This being said, you probably wouldn't be reading this book if you weren't concerned about your body. So, to know for sure whether you need to make some healthy changes, follow the next few tips:

❀ Ask your doctor to tell you where your height and weight fit on the growth chart. Ask to have the measurements explained until you understand them. If you do weigh more than your doctor thinks is healthy, ask if he/she thinks it is fat or muscle (if you're very overweight, it may be obvious that it is fat, and you won't need to ask). This will also encourage your doctor to look at *you* rather than only at the chart.

❀ Do you have large feet or long hands? Are you tall? If you answer yes to these questions, perhaps you have a large body frame. This means the size of your bones is big and long. Since bones are heavy, you may weigh more than you'd imagine, yet not actually be fat. But, if your hands, feet, and height seem average, you need to look for other reasons that you weigh more. If you don't have more muscle, perhaps you do need to lose weight.

❀ If you and your doctor determine it would be better for you to weigh less or have less fat on your body than you do, you need to determine how much weight would be healthy for you to lose. Don't just come up with a goal weight that sounds good to you. The number you decide upon may be unrealistic and impossible to reach. Rather speak to your doctor, a nutritionist, or a fitness expert who specializes in helping teenagers lose weight healthily.

❀ You can also consider using your clothing as a guide for how you look now compared to how you would like to look. This does not mean setting your goal to be a size two or four. In fact, the actual size doesn't matter at all! Rather, concentrate on losing only one clothing size and then speaking with your doctor, a nutritionist, or a fitness expert. Perhaps losing one size will bring you to a healthy weight and you should then focus on maintaining, rather than losing, more weight. If the experts suggest that you keep going, again try only to lose one more size before asking to be checked again. Your goal is not to keep losing weight forever or to look like a fashion model. Rather, it's to reach a realistic weight at which you feel and look healthy according to yourself *as well as to people knowledgeable about the health of girls.* Remember, there *is* such a thing as too thin and it's just as unhealthy as being too fat!

❀ Another way that you can determine a healthy weight for yourself is to use the following formula: If you are five feet tall, a healthy weight is approximately one hundred pounds. Now, add five pounds for every inch you are over five feet. For example, if you are 5'4" then a healthy weight for you is about one hundred and twenty pounds: 100 lbs + [4" x 5 lbs] = 120 lbs. This formula is not exact, but it should give you a good sense of whether you are overweight, and by approximately how much.

Taking Control

For practically all girls reading this book, being overweight is a real problem and one which I will do my best to help you solve! The fact is that your ultimate happiness will come from having the *power and bravery to take control over making healthy decisions for your body and in your life.* If you are overweight, this means taking off some weight or some body fat. You may not have been able to do this until now because you do not yet have the ability to control your eating, exercise, emotions or motivation. This has a lot to do with why it has been so difficult for you to become healthier. Feeling in control can affect many parts of your life, not just your weight and if you feel a lack of control in general it will affect your sense of control around eating and exercise.

So, how much control do you feel in your life? Take the following quiz. Pick the response that is most likely to be the way you'd behave— even if you have never had the particular experience. Be as honest as you can—you don't have to show the results to anyone else. When you're done, use the scoring key to total your points and then check which category you are in. If this is a library book, write your responses and scores on a separate piece of paper.

Dr. Susan's "Am I in Control?" Quiz

 1. When going to a party you

    a. Usually eat a little of the "junk food" and balance it out with healthier choices.

    b. Eat very little all day long so you can eat as much junk as you like at the party, without feeling guilty.

 2. Looking at your naked body you think

    a. I'd like to lose a few pounds, I'm going to come up with a plan to begin gradually eating healthier and exercising a bit more.

b. I wish I could change my body completely—I'm going on a strict diet starting right now and/or I'm going to run a mile every single day until I'm thin.

3. When you are angry with someone you usually

a. Scream first and maybe listen to their side afterwards.

b. Express your feelings, listen to theirs, and then have a discussion.

4. When you look in the mirror you

a. Like some of what you see . . . but everyone has good parts and bad.

b. Always notice your flaws first and can't move past them.

5. You have to miss one day of your new exercise plan so you

a. Tell yourself the plan is ruined so you may as well give it all up.

b. Tell yourself that it's no big deal and pick it up again on the next scheduled day.

6. You have a big test in school that you need to study for, so you

a. Postpone studying until the last minute and then cram, knowing that you haven't studied your hardest.

b. Start a few days before the test by reviewing your notes, figuring out which areas you need to focus on, and then studying calmly and methodically.

7. You just started a new diet and this time you're sure it'll work. In reality

a. You are pretty much able to stick with it for several weeks, just cheating here and there, but then you gradually slip back into your old habits.

b. You stick with it for about a week or less, then you slip up once and decide that it's not worth even trying anymore—at least until the next new diet comes around.

8. When someone walks into your bedroom they are most likely to see

    a. The entire contents of your closets and drawers all over the floor.

    b. That it's quite tidy with just a few things lying around.

 9. You just found out that your crush is taking someone else to the movies. You

    a. Get really depressed and eat for the next few hours to try and help yourself feel better (although you end up feeling guilty about overeating and even worse).

    b. Feel sad, but decide to go to the movies with a group of girlfriends.

 10. Your chore is to clean off the dinner dishes every night, you

    a. Don't love the job, but you do it anyway because you know it's the right thing to do.

    b. Make excuses to get out of doing it as often as you can.

 11. Losing weight is something you

    a. Have been thinking about seriously for a while and you're almost ready to make the commitment to begin working on it.

    b. Try to do most all the time, yet you can't stick with it for more than a few days.

 12. After pigging out you usually feel

    a. Really guilty or angry with yourself—you might eat very little tomorrow to make up for it.

    b. Stuffed but happy—you deserve to splurge once in a while.

The Results

Each "2" means that you are making a controlled and healthy choice in your life—whether it is about eating, exercise or something else. Each

"1" indicates that in some way you feel that you don't have control over your life.

Scoring: Using the scoring key below, calculate your score.

Scoring key

1. a = 2, b = 1	2. a = 2, b = 1	3. a = 1, b = 2	4. a = 2, b = 1
5. a = 1, b = 2	6. a = 1, b = 2	7. a = 2, b = 1	8. a = 1, b = 2
9. a = 1, b = 2	10. a = 2, b = 1	11. a = 2, b = 1	12. a = 1, b = 2

	Answer	Score		Answer	Score
1.			7.		
2.			8.		
3.			9.		
4.			10		
5.			11.		
6.			12.		**TOTAL**
			+		=

Mostly 2s

You're starting with one of the important ingredients necessary to begin making the changes that will help you become healthier and feel better. These results indicate that you are able to make many controlled choices in your life. It's probably just in the areas of eating and exercise that you struggle to be in control. You will find many useful tools throughout this book that will help you learn to use the skills you already possess to gain control in your difficult areas, and so become healthier and feel better about your body.

Mostly 1s

For you, being overweight is probably related to experiencing a lack of control in many areas. Perhaps your life at school or home is hectic or overwhelming, maybe you feel depressed much of the time, or possibly you haven't learned the skills for being in better control of several aspects of your life, including eating and exercise. As you begin reading this book you will find many ways in which you can begin to take control over your eating, exercise, and, most importantly, your feelings. As you learn these new skills you will be able to better control many different aspects of your life. I strongly suspect that gaining control in your life will also make you feel happier in general.

A Mix of 1s and 2s

If you have a fairly balanced number of 1s and 2s, you are likely have some strengths and some weaknesses in the area of control. You will benefit from reading both the Mostly 1s and Mostly 2s sections above because it is likely that while you have some feeling of control in your life, you are still struggling to gain control over your eating and exercise habits—and perhaps other areas too. You will find many parts of this book interesting and useful as you begin your journey towards health and contentment.

No matter which category you are in, you owe it to yourself to be the most confident, happy and satisfied person you can be. As you read on you will learn how to gain control and make changes in your life so that you will notice positive changes in your body. You will also gain an understanding of how to eat and exercise in the healthiest ways possible—without crazy dieting—so that your body will be able to reach its full potential. These tools will give you a lifelong ability to respect and nurture your body. You will learn to have a healthier, better looking body **without** needing to be perfect. In other words, the changes we will strive toward in this book *will take into account* the flaws and imperfections that we all have—now that's a relief!

Help! I'm Not Just Growing Up, I'm Growing Out!

How Puberty Affects Your Weight and Shape

As you know from Chapter 1, learning how to be in control of the choices you make is one of the most important steps to becoming healthier and feeling better about your body. But as you will learn, there are many other factors that impact on your weight. In this chapter we will discuss an important factor over which you actually have very little control—*puberty*. But wait, don't skip this chapter—it's not about breasts, body hair or periods. A parent, health teacher or other adult has probably spoken to you about those things. Or, you may have read a book about your "changing body" (if you haven't heard about any of it, you can go to the library or teen section of the bookstore—you'll find great information there). Rather, this chapter is about understanding how the experience of puberty and how being a preteen and teenager can change your attitude toward food and exercise, which may have resulted in you gaining weight. We'll also discuss what you can do about this, because although you can't control puberty, there are plenty things that you can control—and your health is one of them. After all, growing up doesn't have to mean feeling miserable about how you look. Control is all about knowledge and how you use it, so read on.

Lynn, a high school guidance counselor overheard the following conversation in the cafeteria:

Amanda (age 15): I cleaned out my bedroom drawers yesterday and found photos from my eleventh birthday party. I can't believe how skinny I was! I am totally huge now, compared to then.

Teshia (age 15): You are not! But I know what you mean. I have a pair of jeans everyone signed when I broke my leg three years ago. I tried them on after I'd been dieting for a couple of weeks, and I couldn't even get them over my thighs! I'm as big as a house!

Amanda: I don't think I will ever look that great again, even if I eat nothing and exercise all day long. My body is exploding in all directions—it's out of control!

Abracadabra Presto Chango

So, perhaps you're feeling that puberty has given you a huge and lumpy body. In a strange way, you are right—it has. Your body will definitely look fuller and curvier by the end of puberty. This applies to all girls, whether they are thin, average or overweight. Hormones that your body makes during puberty (growth hormone, estrogen, progesterone, testosterone, and cortisol) cause you to develop curves as well as breasts (and all the other body changing stuff that we're not getting into here). But, the important point is that *it is expected and healthy for a teenage girl to gain weight during puberty.* The exact amount depends upon how much taller you grow and how much your body changes. For example, a girl with smaller breasts may gain less weight than a girl with larger breasts, and a taller girl may gain more weight than a shorter girl. This is totally normal! Take a look at the following list of the way your body changes and how these changes can affect your weight. You will soon understand why all girls can expect to gain body fat and muscle during adolescence:

- You develop breasts (made of fat tissue). This will add weight to your body.

- Your hips widen (preparing your body to carry a baby later in your life), causing normal weight gain.

- Your thighs also increase in size as a natural part of puberty.

- You probably have a growth spurt between the ages of about ten and fourteen. The more you grow the more weight you gain, because the extra bone and muscle will increase your weight. Therefore the taller you are, the more you will and should weigh.

- You get your period (menstruation) which causes your weight to fluctuate monthly depending upon how much fluid your body retains and loses. Of course, fluid retention can also be affected by the weather and exercise (the more you sweat the less water you'll retain and vice versa), your salt intake (too much salt in your diet can cause you to retain fluid), and other variables. Water weight gains or losses are only temporary and don't reflect true weight loss or gain.

- Your stomach may become a bit softer and fuller, causing additional weight gain. Having a *slightly* fuller stomach does not mean that you are fat. In fact, it is a sign that your body is healthy and that it is doing what it should. Of course if you're very overweight, your stomach will be much bigger than is healthy. But even when you reach a healthy weight, you may still have some fat around your stomach. Most girls and women should not expect to have a completely flat stomach.

So now you see that puberty is a time during which you can expect to change your weight and shape. Gaining some weight is not a sign that you're getting fat. it means you're developing in a healthy and normal way. Amanda and Teshia will both need to get used to the idea that they will never look the way they did prior to puberty—they shouldn't want to, because puberty is a an exciting and necessary part of becoming a teenager. But what if your weight gain is above and beyond what is expected during puberty?

What If You've Gained a Lot of Weight?

Although the changes of puberty are normal, you're probably shaking your head and saying "I wouldn't be reading this book if I was just a few pounds overweight!" For some girls, puberty can mean really significant weight gain. They may start out being thin, with a flat figure, and end up having a very full or overweight body! It's likely that this kind of significant weight gain is not just about puberty. It is also related to other things, such as social eating, a busier schedule, and less exercise.

Some girls have a hard time admitting that they are gaining more weight than their bodies need to for health during puberty. Here's Amber's (age 17) story:

66I was always a thin kid. I remember wearing narrow jeans and mini-skirts and I loved tank tops. My parents have pictures of me at the beach posing in bikinis—my body was tiny. Then at about twelve, I started developing. I remember suddenly growing out of my clothes and being angry that my favorite halter-top didn't fit anymore. Then, starting in seventh grade I was allowed to walk home from school with my friends. We'd stop for pizza or candy every day. By the end of the year I'd gained a lot of weight and was wearing at least three, maybe four sizes bigger. But I didn't think anything was wrong. I told myself that I was just "growing up." I think that since my body was developing in so many different ways, I didn't want to admit that I was actually gaining too much weight.**

Like Amber, many girls find that weight creeps up on them without them even realizing it. You hang out with friends and snack more often. Your allowance may be greater, or you get a job to make money—which you spend on food! You may stay up later at night doing homework—and eating. Another factor, which you may not even have thought about, alcohol, can also cause you to gain weight.

Alcohol Adds Inches

Beer, wine coolers, soda, and mixers all have calories, which will definitely pack on the pounds. (Where do you think the term "beer belly" comes from?) The more alcohol you consume, the more weight you'll gain. (Note: this book is not about the really serious problems that alcohol can cause for you. But if you think, or if anyone has suggested, that your alcohol use may be out of control, look in Appendix 2 for ways to get help).

Suddenly Stout

As you can probably see by now, when you combine puberty with increased eating, reduced exercise, and possible alcohol consumption it can be the beginning of a real struggle with weight gain, even for girls that have never struggled with their weight before. This combination represents one of the most common ways for girls to gain weight. We'll call this group of girls Suddenly Stout.

To see if you are a Suddenly Stout sister, take the following short quiz. Check off every sentence that is "a lot like you" or that you "really agree with" (remember to use a separate paper if this is not your book):

- ❏ 1. I used to like clothes shopping, but now I dread it.
- ❏ 2. My mom/aunt/sister is on my back about losing weight or watching what I eat.
- ❏ 3. I've gone up a couple of clothing sizes in the last year.
- ❏ 4. I've been eating a lot of junk food while with my friends, doing homework or watching TV.
- ❏ 5. I haven't been doing much exercise or sporting activities lately, or I'm too busy/tired.
- ❏ 6. My doctor has recently suggested that I start watching my weight.

Scoring: Total up your check marks. If you have more than three checks, you are probably struggling in the Suddenly Stout group.

Flash Forward to College

Even if you only gain a moderate amount of weight through middle and high school, you still need to pay attention to your eating and exercise patterns as you prepare to go to college. Have you heard of the "Freshman Fifteen?" When you go to college you have lots of freedom and new friends. Late night pizza, fraternity parties, and all-you-can-eat cafeterias often cause weight gain (about fifteen pounds) in your first (known as freshman) and even second (sophomore) years of college. These are exactly the same issues as the Suddenly Stout group, simply moved ahead to college!

The "Freshman Fifteen" can become an even greater problem if you're already in the Suddenly Stout group, because you could find yourself significantly overweight by the time you graduate from college. This is not as far away as it may seem, so it's very important to become aware of your eating and exercise habits now. In this way you can change the ones that are causing you to gain more weight than your body needs to get you through puberty and college in a healthy way!

A Plan of Action

Let's review how to maintain or begin to achieve a healthy body weight and shape right through puberty and beyond:

1. Don't increase snacking too much as you enter puberty.

2. Continue to exercise or participate in sports.

3. Consume alcohol with caution.

4. Don't use social gatherings as an excuse to overeat.

5. Instead of using extra money for unnecessary food, spend it on other things, or save it.

6. Keep reading *Dr. Susan's Girls-Only Weight Loss Guide*.

Chubby from Childhood

We've talked a lot about girls who start to gain weight when they become teenagers. But perhaps you fit into a different category. Maybe you were plump or even very overweight before your body felt its first surge of hormones. In fact, if this sounds like you, it wouldn't be surprising because, believe it or not, about one out of every four children is overweight.

Some girls don't have any pictures of themselves as thin, bikini-clad children. In fact, they can only remember being chubby, fat, overweight or heavy. For many girls in this **Chubby from Childhood** group, their childhoods were overshadowed by the feeling that they were different from most other kids because of their weight. If you are in this category, you may have memories of being teased, picked last for a team or told you can't eat another slice of pizza. Girls I've spoken with are often confused about why they've struggled so much and for so long. They want nothing more than to feel that they fit in with their peers, to enjoy clothes shopping, and to not feel guilty when they eat. These are usually sad or angry memories and it can be painful to think of them.

Do you think you may fit into this group? It may be tough to think about sad or frustrated feelings you've had. But try this test and be as honest with yourself as possible. Check off each sentence that you agree with or that seems like you. (remember to use separate paper if this is not your book):

1. I have never liked the doctor because there is always a lecture about my weight.
2. I have never felt really comfortable in clothes that weren't loose fitting.
3. My parents have always tried to get me to eat less junk food or go on a "diet."
4. I was teased about being fat when I was younger (and may still get teased now).
5. I have always been self-conscious about how I look compared to other kids.
6. For some time now I have cried or felt sad about being heavier than most other kids.

Scoring: Count your checks. If you have more than three, you have probably been Chubby from Childhood. This may be difficult to admit, even to yourself. But in order to make changes that will help you feel better about your body, you need to be honest with yourself.

If this is the group you fit into, becoming a teenager might be even tougher for you than for other girls, because the weight gain from puberty will be added to the extra weight you're already carrying. Additionally, possible weight gain from social eating or from not exercising (as we discussed in the Suddenly Stout section) will also affect you.

Like the Suddenly Stouts, Chubby from Childhood girls may have developed a pattern of eating large portions during meals, eating too much junk food, or not exercising enough. The difference is that for the Suddenly Stouts, the pattern began around the same time as they became teenagers. For the Chubby from Childhood group it began many years ago. Being overweight for a long time can result in habits that can be especially hard to break for many reasons.

Challenges to Changing

- It is hard to break unhealthy patterns from childhood because it's the only way you know.
- When you've felt bad about your body for a long time, it's more difficult to become motivated to make changes.
- When you or your parents have tried unsuccessfully for years to help you to lose weight, you may be discouraged and feel like giving up.
- You may come from a family that doesn't focus on healthy eating and exercise. This makes it harder for you to choose a healthy lifestyle, even if you know you should.

❀ You may come from a family that places too much emphasis on healthy eating and exercise. This can also make it tough for you to choose a healthy lifestyle because you feel the urge to reject your family's control over your body.

I think you will agree that being in the Chubby from Childhood group is very difficult, but it's not necessarily much easier to be Suddenly Stout. In fact, girls who need to lose weight (compared to other girls their age and according to their doctors) have a lot in common with each other, no matter which group they're in. Best friends Moira (age 13) a definite Suddenly Stout and Joy (age 13), clearly Chubby from Childhood have more in common with their weight struggles than they have differences.

Weight Worries

by Moira and Joy

We both:

- ❀ Feel unhappy about how we look

- ❀ Want to lose some weight but aren't being successful

- ❀ Need to get motivated to exercise, but are having a hard time doing it

- ❀ Hate feeling deprived of delicious foods

- ❀ Worry that guys won't like us

- ❀ Want to be able to wear the clothes we like

- ❀ Have arguments with our moms about our weight

- ❀ Sometimes feel sad because we don't like our bodies

The bottom line is that no matter which of the "weight struggle" groups you're in, you are not alone. And, like Moira and Joy, it can help to have a friend who feels the same way as you. Even knowing this, many girls still ask the following.

Why Me?

For many girls who struggle with their weight, there is a constant underlying question: Why can't I have a great body without even trying? So many other girls do. In reality, the vast majority of girls and women do not have perfect bodies! To put this in perspective you should know that for every three *billion* women who don't look like supermodels there are only about eight who do! And I bet that of those eight, some have had plastic surgery to bring them closer to some fake ideal of what looking good means to them! The bottom line is that **there is no such thing as a perfect body!** Perfection is not what we are striving to find—health and feeling satisfied with your body are far more important. It is very important to discover what is actually healthy and realistically attainable and not think about a fantasy body that is impossible for you (and three billion other girls and women) to reach.

I Like My Body, But My Doctor Says It's Not That Healthy!

There's a third group of girls that are, or appear to be, content with their bodies even though their doctor/parents/friends are hinting or saying outright that they need to drop a few (or many) pounds. These girls may have gained weight during puberty like the **Suddenly Stout** girls, or they may have been overweight for years like those who are **Chubby from Childhood**.

For example, maybe your doctor has told you that you should lose some weight or maybe you realize that you're heavier than many other girls. In fact, I wonder if someone gave you *Dr. Susan's Girls-Only Weight Loss Guide* hoping that you would realize you need to lose some weight.

But perhaps you don't want to think about this or maybe you're fine with how you look. You may be angry and insulted about their suggestions that you are overweight.

Never the less, if you are getting hints from other people (especially your doctor) that your body isn't healthy, you should probably consider the possibility that this is true—especially if it is coming from people who care about your health. You may fit into a group of girls who are Plump but Pleased. Girls in this category feel comfortable with their bodies even though they are not really at a healthy weight

It can be especially difficult to admit that you need to lose weight when you've been working so hard to have a good body image. However, feeling good about your body when it isn't healthy, is not good for your body. So to check if you are in the Plump but Pleased group of girls, take the following quiz to find out for sure. Check off every sentence that is "a lot like you" or that you "really agree with" (remember to use a separate paper if this is not your book). Be as honest as you can because only you will see your answers:

☐ 1. My doctor and other people have told me that I need to lose weight, but I don't really agree.

☐ 2. I don't care what other people think about my body, I'm fine with what I look like even though I'm heavier than many of my friends.

☐ 3. I would like to lose weight, but I'd never admit it to anyone—they all think I'm happy.

☐ 4. People should like me no matter what I look like and I'm tired of others focusing on weight all the time.

☐ 5. There is a part of me that wishes I could fit into more fashionable clothes, but basically I'm happy with myself.

☐ 6. It's always the really thin girls who constantly talk about losing weight and dieting—I never get into those conversations.

Scoring: Count your checks. If you have more than three, you are probably **Plump but Pleased**. Of course, it is wonderful to feel good about your body—regardless of how it looks, but at the same time it is important to become educated about your health. I'm sure that you have been working hard to feel good about yourself, even though your body may not be as healthy as it should be.

I would suggest that you discuss with your doctor whether there are any medical risks associated with you being overweight. Then you can decide whether you want to make any changes to your eating and exercise habits. Remember: **the best way to have control over your life is to make educated choices.** You may still decide that you're happy with your weight or shape, but you will do so through knowledge rather than ignorance. If you do decide that you would be healthier and happier if you lost some weight, then keep on reading this book and I will show you how to do it.

Is Exercise the Enemy?

For some girls puberty and a developing body may have an unfortunate side-effect. They feel so uncomfortable with their "new" bodies that they choose to give up certain "body moving" activities they loved when they were younger. I bet you know tons of girls (maybe including yourself) who have recently quit ballet, gymnastics, jazz, and figure-skating (just like I did!). Girls often feel that these types of activities require a skinny, light, wiry, delicate, flat, tight, cute, or small body.

In fact it does sometimes seem that those girls who continue successfully in these activities as teens, tend to be petite, thin, and even small-breasted. Now, I am not saying that this is how it **should** be. I'm suggesting that this is how it often **is!** And because of this, many girls who don't fit this "small" figure type begin to feel that they shouldn't be participating. They may even feel embarrassed when they compare themselves to other dancers, skaters or gymnasts.

It's not only activities for petite frames that are forgone. Some girls even give up sports such as basketball, tennis or karate because they don't like to feel their breasts bumping, bouncing or their body sweating. They may also feel awkward, thinking that boys will be watching them, or that the sport is too masculine. Many girls also begin to realize that due to natural ability and talent, other girls happen to be better at a particular sport or activity. They feel embarrassed about this so they give up the activity.

Sometimes, a girl won't make the team because her weight is too high. Perhaps the coach is concerned that she won't be able to run fast enough, or that it will be too much of a strain on her heart. But, this is not always the reason. Ginger, the mother of Anna, one of the girls in my **Girls Advisory Group**, pointed out that teachers and coaches, unfortunately, often contribute to the problem of girls quitting, by favoring and encouraging "smaller" girls. In fact, one dance instructor's commented to Anna's older sister—who is 5'8" and thin—"no one wears a size large leotard."

"How does anyone 5'8", no matter how thin, wear a small or medium?" noted Ginger angrily. "It was impossible for my daughter to meet this 'ideal'!"

Ginger is absolutely right! Of course, we all hope that adults will provide healthy support for girls, but since this is not always the case, it is up to you to develop a confident sense of your own body.

Many dancers, gymnasts, and tennis players, aren't sure how to fit their new bodies into their old activities, so they quit! Unfortunately, girls often don't connect their increasing body size with the reduction in exercise. **When you give up exercise and keep eating the same amount, you also increase your chances of gaining too much weight.** Is there some rule that says you must stop dunking, spinning, flipping or leaping as soon as you no longer have the figure of a child? I say NO, NO, NO! You might never be the best at it, but if you've loved an athletic activity, I challenge you to stick with it even if you'll never be a star and even if you're not as good as some of your friends. Even if you've already stopped, it's not too late to go back to a sport or activity that you love— your body will thank you for it!

If you truly don't want to pursue an old activity, don't give up exercise all together. Instead, replace it with something else. Continuing to exercise is really one of the most important ways you can start to feel better about your body. I'll talk about this in Chapter 10—if you like, you can jump right to it.

Terrific Teen Tip: (Carol, age 16) I started to dance when I was three years old and I loved it. But when I was fourteen, I started comparing myself to the girls in my class. They were mostly tiny, thin, and flat-chested. On the other hand, I was wearing a 34C bra and I was 5'7". I wasn't fat, but I certainly didn't have a ballerina body any more. At first I was really upset because I saw that I would never be a ballerina. But then I realized that wasn't what I wanted anyway. I wanted to go to college and thought that I might be a writer or a fashion designer. But I didn't want to give up dancing all together, because it made me feel good. So I started to take an adult dance class, where everyone's bodies were totally different. I also became an assistant for a nursery school ballet class. I was able to continue dancing without feeling bad about my body. It was the perfect compromise for me!

Now that we've discussed how life as a teenager can cause you to gain weight, make a childhood weight problem even worse, or get you to stop exercising, let's turn to the next chapter and the other important area that can contribute to weight gain—the genes you inherit.

It's All in Your Genes
. . . and I Don't Mean
the Five-Pocket Kind

When You Are Born That Way

Just as you have no control over the fact that your body will change as you go through puberty, you also have little control over the genetic makeup of your body and how the genes you have inherited will affect your body as you go through your teens into adulthood. Your genes are the biological components you get from your parents that, at least partially, make you into who you are. For many girls who feel that they haven't received the most fabulous genes, this is a tough topic. So let's begin to understand it.

We inherit genes from our parents, which is why so much of who we are comes from them. It's impossible to list them all here, but a few of the easily seen ones are: eye and hair color, height, artistic ability, musical ability, certain diseases, and blood type. Three of the most important and sometimes frustrating inherited traits are our body shape, how quickly or slowly our bodies burn food for energy (metabolism), and a tendency to be overweight.

What if I'm Adopted?

Of course, if you're adopted, you may or may not know about your genetic heredity. Your parents might be able to tell you something about what your birth parents looked like, but it's unlikely that they'll have detailed information. If your (adopted) parents are overweight and so are you, it's a good indication that the way your family eats and exercises are the causes of you being overweight, rather than genetics (more on this later in the book). However, if you are overweight but neither of your parents is overweight, you can consider genetics (from your birth parents)—along with some of the other issues we've discussed—as one of the possible reasons for your struggle.

Genes Are Forever

If you've been hearing the phrase, "Do you know you look exactly like your _____ (fill in the blank with mother/father)" since you were young, there is a good chance it is because you've inherited many of the physical traits of that parent. It is important to understand that a **significant** part of what you look like cannot be changed through eating or exercise—no matter how much you diet or work out. It is actually a genetic (physical) part of who you are. You can't change it any more than you can change the size of your feet, your height, sound of your voice, or color of your skin.

For example, if both (or even one) of your parents are big and tall and so are you, you will be more likely to weigh more and look bigger than a girl with average or thin parents. This does not mean you are doomed to a life of being overweight or feeling bad about your body. But you should realize that what may come easily for some may be tougher for you.

For example, from the time Belinda was twelve until she was sixteen, she wanted to lose weight. Her doctor told her that she could benefit from just a little weight loss, although she always felt enormous. Now, at twenty, Belinda has a different view of things. I know that many girls go through what she did, so I asked if she would share her story.

Belinda's Big Body Blues

I hated my body, because by the time I was fourteen I was 5'8" and I wore a size ten shoe. I would never tell anyone what bra size I wore (36D). I wouldn't go clothes shopping with friends because I always felt huge next to them! I would've been embarrassed if they'd known that I wore a size fourteen. I wasn't only bigger than other girls, I was even bigger than practically all the boys, so forget having a boyfriend. I secretly resented my mother because she is 5'10". I got my big size from her! My doctor told me that I was a bit overweight. This just made me feel even larger.

I thought that if I was really careful about what I ate I'd lose weight and become as small and thin as my friends. But it never worked. I'd starve myself for a week or two and lose a few pounds. As soon as I started eating normally again, I'd gain the weight back. Eventually, I gave up and went in the other direction. I started overeating because my attitude was "if I can't be thin, then who cares what I look like!" Of course, I gained even more weight, and then my doctor said I really had to lose weight. I think I would've kept gaining weight if I hadn't met Charlie.

Charlie was my first boyfriend. Now, let me say this up front. I am embarrassed that it took a boy to make me look at my body differently. I wish I'd been able to do it myself, but for some reason I couldn't. That's why I'm sharing this story with you, so you don't have to wait for a boy to tell you that you're beautiful.

I met Charlie the summer after I graduated from high school—we both worked at the town pool. He was nineteen, really cute, and tall—perfect for me!! He asked me out after we'd spent an afternoon painting a fence together. I was surprised because I didn't think any boy would be interested in me. After we'd been going out a month, I finally had the nerve to ask Charlie if he thought I should lose weight. He said that he thought it would be good for me to lose some weight, but that being tall and having big feet is who I am and that would never change—no matter how much weight I lost. We talked for a while and I learned three things that I will remember for the rest of my life:

1. Being tall and big doesn't make someone any less pretty, appealing or interesting than anyone else.
2. Beauty really is in the eye of the beholder—so make sure that when you **behold** *yourself* you see someone beautiful.
3. Being a big person isn't the same as being overweight. No matter what genes you have, you should respect your body and yourself by eating and exercising in a healthy way so that even if you're big, you're not overweight.

I finally came to accept that I wasn't unlucky for getting my mother's genes. I started eating better and exercising more. Now my doctor says my weight is perfect for my height and body shape. There is still a small part of me that would like to be skinny, small-breasted, and shorter. But I know that it's just not who I am. I am proud of myself—I'm strong, athletic, smart, and a pretty good pianist. I wish I'd been able to accept myself in high school because it would've saved me a lot of grief, not to mention the weight gain that came from disliking myself so much.

Well, that's my story. "What about Charlie?" you're wondering. We broke up half way through my first year at college.

We were at different schools and the distance was difficult. But I've had a couple of boyfriends since then, and now I'm going out with someone terrific—and tall, of course! I really like myself now, and it shows.

Don't Be Disappointed

It took Belinda a long time to realize that her genes played an important part in what she looks like and that being tall and having big body parts is separate from being overweight. In fact, there are many different body shapes that can make you feel that since you don't have a perfect body you may as well just let yourself gain weight. For example, are you short and stocky? Are you pear-shaped with a heavy bottom and small top? Are you very tall, with wide hips and large breasts? Having one of these body types may make you feel that you can never look good. In reality, as Belinda discovered, your body type has little to do with being healthy or being at a good weight. So, once you have an accurate view of your body type, you will be able to develop realistic expectations for what your body could and should look like at its healthiest. *Like Belinda, it is likely that even when you are very healthy, you will not have a perfect body because, as you know, the vast majority of us don't.* This is important to think about as you continue to read and apply the ideas in this book. This way you won't be disappointed with the results of all your hard work. Remember that being healthy and looking good are not about perfection, but about making the most of your body, no matter what your body type.

So What Is Your Body Type?

In the 1940s a psychologist named William Sheldon figured out that there are three main body types. These are basically genetically predetermined and a part of what makes you, wonderful you!! The three types are: ectomorph, endomorph and mesomorph (by the way, morph means "body").

An ectomorph typically has the following characteristics: thin, tall, long arms and legs, narrow shoulders and hips, is less muscular, and has trouble gaining weight.

An endomorph has these characteristics: rounder-shaped, not very muscular, wider hips (sort of pear shaped), larger breasts, a soft body, and a tendency to gain weight.

A mesomorph's characteristics are: muscular, with broader hips and shoulders, loses and gains weight easily, and is not soft or flabby.

Some girls fall clearly into one of these three groups. However, many more girls are a combination of one or more of these groups. For example, it is possible to be somewhat round (endomorphic) and also be muscular (mesomorphic). You might also be muscular (mesomorphic) and also tall and thin (ectomorphic). You could have long arms and legs (ectomorphic) with few defined muscles (mesomorphic).

When you are overweight and therefore carrying extra fat on your body, you may look more like an endomorph than anything else. However, body types are not determined by how much fat you have on your body, because this can change if you lose or gain weight. Rather, they tell you what you should look like once you are at a good weight for your body. If you are an endomorph, for example, you will never be slim, with narrow hips and a tiny bottom—no matter how much you exercise or eat healthily. Rather, you will need to learn how to make your body the healthiest it can be, but have realistic expectations for what you will actually look like when you are at a healthy weight for your height and body shape. Of course exercise can modify your body somewhat.

In other words, knowing your type will help you to figure out what to expect when you look in the mirror at a healthy weight and shape. Take Belinda, she's a mesomorph. That means she'll never be small and thin, no matter how much she diets or exercises. She can also expect to weigh more than her friends because she's tall and muscular. And while you probably know that the taller you are the more you should weigh, here's an interesting point—muscle also makes you weigh more because it is heavier than fat! So, you can see it would be unhealthy for Belinda to even try to look smaller or weigh less. She would be depriving her body of what it needs to continue growing healthily.

Another reason to know your body type is because as you begin making changes in your lifestyle to lose weight or change your shape, you should know what you can realistically expect to look like when you've achieved your goals. This way you won't be disappointed that, despite all your hard work, you still don't look like a supermodel. Some body types are naturally bigger, softer or rounder than others. In order to begin on the path to changing your body, you need to know your body type.

So now, I've got you wondering, "what's my body type?" Okay, take this quiz by circling True or False below (don't forget to use separate paper if this is a library book).

What's Your Type?

1. People often use the word "athletic" to describe my body.

TRUE   FALSE

2. My shoulders are definitely narrower than my hips—I'm sort of pear-shaped.

TRUE   FALSE

3. My friends sometimes say they're jealous of my flat stomach.

TRUE   FALSE

4. I have strong arms and well-defined shoulders compared to other people.

TRUE   FALSE

5. I have trouble losing weight, even when I really try.

TRUE   FALSE

6. My calf muscles are well-developed.

TRUE   FALSE

7. I sometimes wish my whole body was more developed—it's sort of flat.

TRUE   FALSE

8. My body is soft and not really muscular.

TRUE   FALSE

9. I must have a "fast metabolism" because I really don't gain weight even when I pig out.

TRUE   FALSE

10. My arms and legs are long and thin.

TRUE   FALSE

11. I have a muscular stomach, shoulders, and chest compared to other girls.

TRUE   FALSE

12. I have larger breasts than many of my friends.

TRUE   FALSE

13. I usually have to buy "slim" or "small" size clothes or they will be too big on me.

TRUE   FALSE

14. My waist is smaller than my shoulders and hips.

TRUE   FALSE

15. My thighs and upper arms are softer and rounder than those of other girls.

TRUE   FALSE

16. My body is naturally in good shape.

TRUE   FALSE

17. I am not muscular at all.

TRUE   FALSE

18. I think I have been chubby or fat my whole life.

TRUE   FALSE

19. My body is straight up and down, not really curvy.

TRUE   FALSE

20. I would describe myself as strong and energetic.

TRUE   FALSE

21. I have a very curvy body.

TRUE   FALSE

Scoring

- If you said "true" to 2, 5, 8, 12, 15, 18 or 21, you have **endomorphic** characteristics
- If you said "true" to 3, 7, 9, 10, 13, 17, or 19, you have **ectomorphic** characteristics
- If you said "true" to 1, 4, 6, 11, 14, 16 or 20, you have **mesomorphic** characteristics

You have *characteristics* of a particular body type rather than having that body type because, as we discussed, many people don't fit perfectly into one type or another. So, if your scores showed that you have characteristics of two or more categories, it's not unusual. See which categories (it may be two) that appear most frequently in your scores. This will help you determine your general body type. For example, when I took the test, I said "true" to five mesomorphic responses, three endomorphic responses, and one ectopmorphic response. That means that I am mostly a mesomorph with a little bit of endomorph. My one ectomorphic response doesn't really mean anything. So if you answer "true" only once, it isn't really a good reflection of your true body type. The most common "mix" is a meso-endo (like me!), so if you find that you are this, or any other combination, use the knowledge to know your body's potentials as well as its limitations.

Self Acceptance Is a Must

Okay, so you've figured out your body type and I bet you're not an ectomorph, since they're the ones that don't gain weight. You probably wouldn't be reading this book if that were your issue.

It may be difficult to accept that your body type means that you may never be a size four or look as great in a bikini as your ectomorphic friend. Perhaps halter-tops and short shorts won't be your thing; or maybe tiny mini-skirts and tank tops will never flatter your shape even when your body is at its absolute best! Is this tough to hear? When I was a teenager, I refused to accept it. I was sure that when I finally got to the "perfect weight" I would look amazing in everything I put on. I couldn't have been more wrong! It took me a long time—into adulthood actually—to come to terms with my shape. At my perfect weight I still can't put on absolutely all clothes and look great, and I'll never, ever, ever be a size four! But now I know that my body is the healthiest it can be and I feel good about myself. Of course, getting to this point of self acceptance can be frustrating and upsetting if you have a sister or mother or even friends that got the "good genes." But keep on reading this book because I'll give you different ways to help yourself not only look, but feel better.

By now you know that there is no such thing as a perfect body. Rather, puberty and genetics will largely determine what will be healthy for your body when it is at its best. Your healthiest weight for your height, body type, and age may not mean that you will look good in skimpy clothes or tiny sizes. So you will have to work hard to realize that your goal is NOT to be able to dress in certain clothes to feel you have succeeded. Instead, you should realize that:

> Looking and feeling good are not about what your body can wear, but about how much you love and care for your body.

You can begin to feel better about your body right now by recognizing that no matter what your body type, there are so many different types of clothes, it is almost impossible NOT to find styles of pants, tops, bathing suits, and workout clothes that will look good on you once you're at a healthy weight and shape for *your body*.

Of course, you probably realize that until you get to this point (and even when you do), it probably won't be simple to feel good about your body even though you're trying to look and feel your best. As you're working toward reaching better health (which you will reach if you follow everything in this book), you may need to fight against many different pressures from friends, family, the media, fashion, and even guys, to look and feel a certain way about your body. In the next chapter, we will explore the different pressures and subtle messages that can make you feel so bad that they interfere with your ability to keep working toward looking and feeling better. I will help you to fight against these pressures and negative messages.

Four

From Friends to Family to Fashion: Fighting to Feel Fabulous

Friends Can Help or Hurt Your Body Image

Most friendships will help you feel good about yourself. Friends stick together through good times and bad. They also help give you a secure and safe feeling when you step out into the world of school and socializing. However, you may not realize it, but when you are overweight some interactions with friends can actually interfere with you becoming and feeling healthier. In some cases, these interactions can also really stress your friendship. Check out these friendship factors to figure out how to handle them effectively.

Friendship Factor #1: My Thin Friend Is Obsessed with Her Weight

"Tara, who knew she was overweight, began to dread spending time with her best friend, Lynne. That's because Lynne talked nonstop about wanting to lose weight and go on a diet. In reality, Lynne looked fine—so Tara couldn't help thinking that Lynn must really think Tara was huge! Tara was even embarrassed to tell Lynne that she was trying to lose weight. She thought that if she mentioned it, then Lynne would simply talk even more about losing weight herself, without realizing how awkward this was for Tara."

After talking to many girls, I have discovered that Tara's dilemma is quite common. Some overweight girls believe that their slimmer friends don't realize they are being insensitive. Others believe that a friend may talk like this on purpose to try and motivate them (the overweight friend) to become more aware of her own body so she will try to lose weight. Still others think that a thin girl might talk about weight loss in front of a truly overweight friend because she has low self-esteem and somehow pretending she needs to lose makes her feel better about herself. She knows that, in reality, she doesn't really have to lose weight when compared to her friend. In this last situation, I'm not sure that I would consider the thin girl a true friend if she needs to make someone else feel bad so she can feel good.

No matter what the reason for your slim friend talking about her weight constantly, the conversation is not healthy for your friendship, if it makes you feel worse about yourself. It is therefore important for you to speak to your friend about how you are feeling. This may not be easy, but here are some steps for how to make the conversation go a bit more smoothly.

1. Ask your friend if you and she could find a quiet time to talk privately.

2. Tell her that you value her friendship, which is why you want to talk to her about how you are feeling.

3. Explain that for some time now you haven't been feeling good about your body, but you are taking steps to lose weight and feel better.

4. Now, tell her that you've noticed that whenever you and she are together, she talks a lot about dieting and losing weight. Explain that since she is much slimmer than you, it makes you imagine that she must be thinking about how overweight you are.

5. You should also say that it makes you feel unwilling to share your concerns about your own body, even though you would really like to be able to do so. Add that you will need a lot of support and help as you try to lose weight, but that having a slim friend talk about weight loss all the time makes you frustrated and upset.

6. Ask your friend why she feels so bad about her own body. Perhaps you will find out something about her that will make your friendship closer. Maybe you'll realize that although you have a real weight problem, she also has struggles with her body image and self-esteem. Hopefully, you'll be able to help each other.

7. If you're brave enough, ask your friend to tell you how she feels about you being overweight. Explain that you're trying really hard to lose weight and become healthier. Ask her for her help and support.

8. Then, ask your friend if she could try to talk less about dieting and weight loss. Agree that you will both talk to each other about how you feel and that you will try to help each other feel better.

Terrific Teen Tip: After Linda and her friend Lana (both age 14) had an open conversation about weight loss and their bodies, they made a pact not to talk negatively about their weight, clothes, and bodies when they get together. Now, instead, they focus on other things—like boys (of course), homework, and the latest movie. They've agreed that once a week they will get together and each one will have exactly 5 minutes to complain about her own body—but that's it! They feel that their friendship has become more interesting and meaningful since making the pact. They highly recommend it for other teenage girls.

9. If, no matter what you try, you can't stop a friend's negative self-talk, you may have to consider spending less time with her. Instead, hang out with girls who value more diverse and positive conversations.

Friendship Factor #2: Jabs of Jealousy

Debbie (age 17), who is overweight, had a dilemma while trying on her prom dress for her friend, Sue. "Sue and I had checked out every store in the mall for dresses. Finally, Sue found one she loved and it looked great on her. But when she came out of the fitting room I got this urge to tell her it didn't flatter her. Why did I have such an awful response?"

Sometimes, when you don't feel good about your body and you're hanging out with a friend who looks great, your criticism may be the result of jealousy towards your friend. For example, Megan (age 14) admitted that when her friend, Katie, wore a new pair of jeans to school, she told Katie they were too tight and made her look fat.

Actually, Katie's pants looked awesome. It's just that I could never wear them because I'm about thirty pounds heavier than Katie. I hated her for a minute because I was jealous, and it came out in a really mean way. I felt bad afterwards, but I couldn't tell Katie because I was too embarrassed.

Megan and Debbie's feelings are not unusual. Have you ever criticized a friend because you just couldn't stand how *good* she looked? It's a strange feeling—part of you feels that if you criticize her *she'll think* she looks bad, and another part feels that the criticism is justified because she's just so perfect, she deserves it. But, yet another part of you realizes that criticizing her doesn't make you feel better about yourself and it may even make you feel worse knowing you're hurting a friend. It's not easy to get these kinds of feelings under control, but since it's not okay to be mean to a friend, here are some suggestions for how to deal with them.

→ Admit honestly to yourself—say it out loud or write it in your journal—that you are jealous of your friend's body or the way she can wear certain clothes that you can't wear.

→ When you get the urge to criticize her, count to fifty, then ask yourself if you *really* want to say it. If you still do, ask yourself if the criticism is about feeling jealous. If it is, don't say it!

→ If your friend asks your opinion about clothes, be honest and don't allow jealousy to take over when you're giving an opinion.

→ If it's difficult for you to go shopping with a friend because it evokes jealousy in you, don't go!

→ If she is a good friend, maybe you can tell her how you feel and ask her to be sensitive about your feelings when you and she are discussing clothes.

But, what are you to do with these feelings? *Why* are you jealous of your friend? Take an honest look at the parts of yourself you don't like. For example, does your friend have a flatter stomach, thinner thighs, or an overall better body than you? Do you wish you had her breasts, arms or butt? Now, ask yourself the following important question: **Do you have control over changing the parts of your body that you don't like?**

If you've already read Chapters 2 and 3, then you probably know the answer to this question. If you haven't read them yet, then stop right here and go back and read these chapters before you continue here.

Now you know that although you can't control every aspect of your body, you have a great deal of control over whether or not you are overweight. So, stop feeling sorry for yourself and jealous of her, and start working toward feeling better about yourself. Take action! Read the rest of this book to discover the many ways you can start feeling better about YOU, without having to criticize a friend.

Additionally, take a careful look at your friend. It's possible that she's genetically blessed with a perfect figure (see Chapter 3), but it's also very likely that the lifestyle choices she makes contribute to the way she looks. For example, if your friend exercises, and makes healthy food choices most of the time, you have no reason to be jealous. Instead, begin taking steps to make your body the best it can be. This doesn't mean going on a strict diet or exercising all day. You may never look like your friend because no two people can look exactly alike—and don't forget genetics. But if you're healthy and active, you'll begin to like your own body and you won't feel the need to compare it to anyone else.

Friendship Factor #3: My Friend Is Always Criticizing Me

"Isabelle (age 15) was feeling really upset about her relationship with her friend Ashley. "Ashley has made it clear that she thinks I'm fat," explained Isabelle, "and I agree because my doctor has told me the same thing. But Ashley is always telling me to eat less and to stop eating junk food. She also tells me that I need to have more will power and that guys won't like me if I don't lose weight. I'm beginning to dread spending time with Ashley because I feel constantly criticized by her."

What if, whenever you spend time with your friend, she's always criticizing you? You may be overweight and you may not be happy with your body right now, but if a friend is always critical, you shouldn't just accept it. You owe it to yourself (and your body) to confront your friend about how she makes you feel. It's tough to have a discussion about such an awkward topic, but since it's so important, here's a "cheat sheet." Of course, this may not be exactly how it goes, but remember, no matter how you look, self-respect should guide you to make sure you don't let your friends treat you badly. Set up a time for you and your friend to talk. Then begin like this:

You: There is something important I want to discuss with you. Remember the other day when _____ (fill in with a description of the event, including what she said).

Her: Yes, I remember (or something similar).

You: Well, it really hurt my feelings when you said _____ (fill in the blank). I appreciate your advice and suggestions, but when you criticize me or my body, it feels really bad.

Her: (hopefully) Wow, I didn't realize you felt like that. I'm really sorry.

OR (hopefully not) I didn't criticize you, you're just too sensitive.

You: Thanks for listening, I'm so glad I can talk to you about my feelings. I would really appreciate your support now, because I am trying to lose weight and feel better about my body.

OR I guess we just don't see this the same way, but the next time we go shopping, I'll point it out to you. But if I can't feel comfortable, maybe we shouldn't shop together again.

Terrific Teen Tip: Carla (age 16) says that when she argues with a friend, it is less likely to become a huge fight if she talks about her own feelings rather than blaming her friend. For example, Carla will say "I often feel criticized when we go shopping together," rather than "you always criticize me when we go shopping. She says that using the word "I" rather than "you" always works for her. She thinks you should definitely try it, too.

Now, here's the hard part. Although she sounds critical, it's possible that your friend has a genuine concern about how you look (for example, maybe you've chosen an outfit that doesn't look good on you). She may not know how to tell you tactfully, but being hurt or angry won't make you look any better in the clothes. So, when you get the feeling your friend (or for that matter anyone else) is trying to tell you to rethink an outfit, try *this* on for size:

1. Take a careful look in the mirror, from all sides.

2. Ask your friend to be specific about what she doesn't like.

3. Try not to be defensive. Instead evaluate the comments with an open mind.

4. Try on other outfits to make a comparison.

5. If you still decide you like the outfit ask for a second opinion, and look at yourself in it a few more times.

6. If, after all this, you're still sure you love it, wear it proudly and feel good about yourself!

Your friends aren't the only ones who can make it a challenge to feel good while you're trying to lose weight. Sometimes family members can also make you feel upset or angry. Read on to see what I mean.

The Family Factor

Here's a quick quiz—answer yes or no to the following questions:

1. Do your parents watch everything you eat with a critical eye?

2. Are there always "special low-fat snacks" in the house, especially for you because your parents don't think you should eat the cookies?

3. Do you have a thin mother or sister who can eat everything and never gain a pound (and is this talked about all the time)?

4. Do you and your mom fight a lot about what you're eating or wearing or why you're not exercising more than you are?

5. Is your mom always trying to find clothes that flatter your figure—even when you don't ask?

6. Do your parents try to get you to take walks around the block with them, saying *they* need the exercise (yeah right!)?

If you answered yes to more than one or two of these, you're in the Family Stress Zone (FSZ). The FSZ is when your weight, what you eat, how much you exercise, and how you look compared to other people in the family has become a family "issue." And that means big stress for you. It's difficult enough to be overweight, but when the whole family focuses on it and tries to "fix" or "help" you, it can make you feel even worse. Never the less, in most cases, people (especially your parents) are just trying to help you. So how do you get out of the FSZ?

Unlike situations with friends you can't just stop hanging out with members of your family if you don't like how they are behaving. Instead, you have to figure out how to benefit from their help without becoming upset. You also need to teach them how to help you without hurting your feelings. Let's look at the six quiz issues again and I'll give you some tips for how to deal with the issues in a way that will help you exit the FSZ!

#1: Your Parents Watch Everything You Eat with a Critical Eye

Do you ever have the urge to eat second helpings or junk food when your parents aren't around? If you answered "Yes" to this question, it is probably because one or both parents watches what and how much you eat, somehow communicating that they are not happy with your eating choices. Actually, your parents are not happy with the fact that you are overweight. If you were at a healthier weight, they probably wouldn't pay much attention to what you eat. To try to get your parents to stop studying your eating habits you will need to do the following:

❋ Explain to them (calmly!) that it makes you uncomfortable and is causing you to eat secretly, rather than to eat more healthily.

❄️ Ask them to voice their concerns about your weight once—in a letter (or email). Promise that if it is written with love and sensitivity, you will read it. Assure them that after they write the letter, they do not have to (and you do not want them to) focus on your eating habits.

❄️ Explain that no matter how much they worry, only you can control what and how much you eat. Hopefully, you can also tell them that you're starting to learn how to be healthier by reading *Dr. Susan's Girls-Only Weight Loss Guide.*

❄️ Ask them to read the "Note to Parents" in the front of this book.

#2: There Are Always "Special Low-Fat Snacks" in the House, Especially for You Because Your Parents Don't Think You Should Eat the Cookies

Many of the issues from Question #1 apply here as well. In addition, if your parents are buying special snacks because *they* think you should be eating them, you can (without yelling!) explain the following:

❄️ You need to have control over what you choose to eat or not eat. You would appreciate it if they would not make these decisions for you.

❄️ Depriving yourself of certain foods (like cookies) will only make you crave them more and then binge (eat huge amounts) on them. As you read this book, you are (hopefully) trying to learn to eat all foods in moderation, without eating too much of any foods (ask them to read Chapter 6, Predictable Family Patterns, and Chapter 7, On a Diet . . . Off a Diet—The Rocky Road to a Not so Healthy Body).

❄️ If they're choosing to have certain foods in the house, it should be for everyone, not just you. It makes you feel bad to be singled out.

❄️ You would be grateful if they would buy certain foods when you request them and as you learn to eat more healthily from this book.

#3: You Have a Thin Mother or Sister Who Can Eat Everything and Never Gain a Pound

It can be very difficult and even make you feel jealous when you are overweight and your mom or sister is the opposite. This can become even worse when they are trying to help you lose weight, because they could never understand how difficult it is for you! However, it is important to keep in mind that they are trying to do what they think will be most helpful for you. You can help yourself feel less resentful and jealous by doing the following:

- Remind yourself that different body types are just a fact of life—your family member isn't trying to hurt you by being thin. Accept your body type and work with it.

- Pay attention to whether the slimmer member of your family eats better or exercises more than you do. Be honest with yourself about this. Then, ask yourself what you can do to make the best of your body by continuing to follow the eating and exercise plans in this book.

- Talk to your mom or sister about how you feel. This may not be easy, but it will be well worth it. They may not know how bad you feel when you compare yourself to them. The knowledge will help them to become more sensitive to how they talk to and around you.

- If necessary, speak with a counselor or other trusted adult about your jealousy.

#4: You and Your Mom Fight a Lot about What You're Eating or Wearing or Why You're Not Exercising More Than You Are

Fighting between mothers and overweight daughters (even when mom is also overweight) is the most common issue I see! In order to end the fighting, both you and your mom will have to take responsibility for making changes in the way you talk to each other. I'd suggest that you ask her to read this section with you.

* Ask your mom to do her best to stop making ANY comments about your weight, eating or exercise.

* In place of her comments, she should write you a letter (see Question #1) outlining all her concerns. This way she'll feel confident that you know clearly how she feels. You can then decide what to do with the information.

* If your mom slips up and comments, criticizes or suggests anything, you need to STAY CALM. Yelling, cursing, throwing a tantrum, or crying will only make things worse and guarantee a fight. Instead, politely remind her that you are working on becoming healthier—and mean it!

#5: Your Mom Is Always Trying to Find Clothes That Flatter Your Figure—Even When You Don't Ask

This one is very simple—shop alone and ask your parents not to bring clothes home for you. If you are not quite old enough to shop alone, you can still ask your parents not to bring clothes home for you. You can also ask them to wait for you to pick clothes off the racks and store shelves, rather than bringing you clothes that they think will "flatter your body." Of course, since your parents are buying your clothes, you may still have to consider their opinion—it's not fair to expect them to spend their money on clothing that they strongly dislike. You may have to compromise, finding clothes that you like and that they don't hate.

#6: Your Parents Try to Get You to Take Walks Around the Block with Them, Saying *They* Need the Exercise

If your parents are always trying to get you to exercise, it's probably because they are concerned that you aren't doing it yourself. The easiest solution is to begin exercising (read Chapter 10). Then they'll have nothing to complain about. If you're not ready to do this yet, perhaps you should consider taking them up on the offer to "walk around the block." If you don't enjoy their company, perhaps you could just put some good music in your earphones and walk around the block yourself. Hey, guess what—now you're exercising. I'm trying to say you shouldn't fight them on this one. Exercise is one of the most important things you can do for your body, your brain, and your feelings. A walk around the block will make you feel good.

So now you've figured out how to cope with family stresses, but how do you cope with all the media messages out there that tell you being healthy isn't enough—that you must be skinny to be happy. This pressure to be skinny and perfect is enough to make anyone give up even trying to become healthy.

Movies, Magazines, and Models—The Media Blitz

"Marika (age 15) loved fashion magazines, especially looking at the beautiful, unbelievably thin models. But after reading one of these, Marika would always feel hopeless—she could never look like that so why even bother trying to lose the weight that her doctor had recommended she lose."

Open any fashion or teen magazine, click on the TV, or walk through a department store. The images of impossibly thin models can overwhelm you. But did you know that most models are thinner than 98 percent of American girls and women. Think about that statistic. It means that it's almost impossible to look like a model. Yet most teenage girls (whether or not they are overweight) constantly compare themselves to these models and even use them as the ideal for which to strive.

In fact, many fantasize about what their lives would be like if they had the body of a super model (admit it, you've done it!). Marika shared her fantasy:

> **"I'd** be rich, glamorous, famous, and, of course, the boys would be falling all over me. If I looked like a supermodel, there'd be nothing stopping me. I feel it would solve all my problems. And, I'd be able to eat what ever I wanted without worrying!**"**

The power of TV can also be overwhelming. It draws you in, and it's so easy to get lost in the characters. Week after week, you see their lives unfolding. They're gorgeous, with fabulous bodies, sporting expensive clothes. In fact, if you really think about it, some of the shows you love to watch don't have great plots or story lines, but they do have great looking girls and women. They seem to lead much more interesting, exciting, and dramatic lives than the rest of us—and they always get the gorgeous guy. And somehow it all seems to be tied up into how they look and what they wear. It's very seductive and it's understandable that you might wish, pray or fantasize about being one of these "chosen" few.

But there's a much bigger picture to look at. And as a teenager or preteen, you're certainly old enough to become educated about what motivates the idealistic body images portrayed by the media.

It's a Matter of Money

Glamour, beauty, and sexy bodies sell magazines, movies, TV shows, and clothes. Take your favorite TV show. You watch it because it's exciting and fun. But if the actors had the average looks and body types, and if they wore boring clothes and had boring lives, it's likely you wouldn't be as interested, right? Well, chances are you wouldn't be the only one feeling this way. In fact, most people wouldn't be interested. But if no one watched, then the show would be a failure. Advertisers won't pay lots of money to be on a show that no one is watching. And it is these ads (the ones that interrupt the show every ten minutes or so) that pay to keep the television networks on the air. In other words, if you haven't figured it out yet, fabulous bodies and looks keep TV shows on the air, which keeps the advertisers paying, which keeps the networks going, and so on.

It's the same with movies. People are more willing to pay more money to see glamorous stars and fabulous looking heroes, than they are to see regular people like you and me. Haven't you noticed that the heroine is almost always the prettiest woman with the best body? This is no accident. Movie producers and directors know that hot bodies make big bucks!

What about clothing models? By now you've probably figured it out—everyone is more willing to buy clothes if they look great on the model. Why is that? Well, remember that fantasy about being glamorous and having tons of boyfriends? When we see a gorgeous model in a beautiful outfit we think "Maybe if I wear that outfit, I'll be just as gorgeous as her, and then I'll have her fabulous life too." That fantasy tempts us to buy the clothes, which is exactly what the designers and stores want us to do. You see, the fashion industry *also* knows that gorgeous bodies bring in the cash!

So you see, while it can be discouraging to look at these perfect bodies, and wish you could look like them, (especially if you're overweight), the reality is that barely anyone actually looks like them. Very often, even *they* don't look like them.

Fabulous but Fake

Do you ever wonder how those models and actors get to look like that and if they are really happier than everyone else? Some of it is genetics—they're just naturally thin, pretty or sexy. But actually, the media controls a great part of the way these women and girls look.

→ Fact one: They spend hours a day putting on makeup, dressing, and doing their hair to look just perfect. There are constantly make-up artists and hair stylists hovering around to touch them up.

→ **Fact two:** They spend even more time exercising to keep their bodies in perfect shape—it could be more than four hours a day.

→ **Fact three:** They diet and deprive themselves in an extreme (and very unhealthy) way, for weeks or months at a time.

→ **Fact four:** Their lives are hardly ever as glamorous as they appear to be on TV, in magazines or in movies. No matter what they look like, they have the same ups and downs as everyone else.

→ **Fact five:** Television, the movies, and modeling are VERY competitive so only a tiny minority make really "big bucks." The rest struggle most of their lives and aren't especially successful.

→ **Fact six:** They have the same problems with guys as you do—they just don't talk about it.

→ **Fact seven:** Magazines airbrush out imperfections from the photos of models to make them look perfect, because even models don't have perfect features.

→ **Fact eight:** Many models and actors were just regular kids like you. They worked very, very hard and sacrificed a lot. Most of them don't have time for friends or family; they may not have even finished high school or college. But these were choices they made to become successful.

→ **Fact nine:** Models have very short careers because their success is about their looks. How would you feel if you were a has-been by the age of twenty-five? That's the way it is with modeling.

→ **Fact ten:** Actors and models have very long days and work really hard. They typically wake up at four or five in the morning in order to have enough time to exercise, put on makeup, and get ready for work. They often don't end their days until ten or eleven at night. Remember, things are not always as glamorous as they seem.

Now you have the facts! But even knowing that the media promotes impossible ideals, may not be quite enough to stop you from sometimes wishing you had the perfect body or ideal life. So here are some tips to help you keep things in perspective when you're feeling especially vulnerable to the media blitz.

- Only two out of every one hundred girls and women could ever have a body like a model, even when she's at a healthy weight and shape. So when you're feeling bad, remember, your goal is to strive to be the healthiest you possibly can be—not to look perfect!

- Having a perfect body *does not* guarantee you will be popular, famous or successful. There are many other factors such as talent, luck, and experience that are even more important. So it's important to nurture all parts of your life—academics, music, sports, art, dance, friendship, and any other interests or talents you may have. Of course, at the same time, you want to keep working on becoming healthier.

- The department store mannequins may be thin, but—reality check—they're not even *real*. A woman made from plastic doesn't count at all, so don't even bother comparing yourself to her (it?)

- When you see your favorite actress, focus on what you love about her besides her looks—you'll be surprised to find that she has many other attractive characteristics (personality, sense of humor, sensitivity). If she didn't have them, you wouldn't like her nearly as much, despite her great body.

- If you're feeling especially angry, write a letter to your favorite magazine. Tell them you want to see models that more closely resemble reality! Also, a small number of fashion magazines have been trying to use models with more "real" bodies. Find these and spend your money on them instead. In addition, check out other ways you can voice your opinion (the Internet is a good place to start). Make it a cause and rally your friends!

Of course, realizing that you will probably never look like a supermodel or movie star doesn't mean that you should give up on looking and feeling the best that you can be. Rather it means that you should have realistic goals that fit your body type (did you take the body-type quiz in Chapter 3?) Keep reading and soon you will start figuring out how to reach those goals.

Staying in Style May Seem Stressful

❋ Everyone was wearing tiny T-shirts but when Cindy tried one on, it looked awful on her. Her stomach bulged and her breasts looked huge. Disappointed, she quickly took it off.

❋ Linda searched the mall for a dress to wear at the dance. That evening, Linda sat on her bed and cried for an hour. She hadn't found anything stylish that looked good on her. To make matters worse, she felt fat and ugly.

There's always something new in style, no matter what the season. It could be tank tops, jeans, leggings, scarves, platform shoes, Capris or tiny T-shirts. And when it's **in** it's **everywhere**! Every store window, catalogue, magazine, TV show, in your school, and on your friends. And if you don't own at least one of what's *in*, you feel like you're *out*. But because fashions often look best on slim people (as we discussed above), then when you're overweight, like Cindy and Linda, the style of the moment is often not flattering to your body. When this happens you may get depressed and angry, yelling at your mom in the store, sulking or crying. One of the most difficult things about being a teenager is feeling you don't fit in with your friends. And being in style is definitely at the top of the list for making you feel you fit in.

But here's another way to look at it: you have started working toward feeling better about your body, right? That's why you're reading this book. As you become healthier, you will definitely find that there are more clothes in which you will feel comfortable and look good.

Of course, as we discussed in Chapter 3, genetics plays a role in your body's shape, so even when you're at your best, you may not look great in every single fashion. This is true for most girls—they look good in some styles and not others. So look around you—really look—you will notice that most girls will stick with their old favorites. They'll probably wear something "stylish" only once in a while. So even if the "in" style doesn't flatter your body type, no one will notice, and before you know it something new will be in every store window.

Nevertheless, when you're overweight, it can feel like nothing ever looks good on you! And weight loss doesn't seem to be coming fast enough, even though you are working at it. Have you ever bought an outfit because you loved how it looked on the model or your best friend or on the hanger? Maybe you even tried it on in the store and didn't like the way it looked, but you bought it anyway. If you've done this you're not alone. And *you* know that sometimes you buy an outfit, even if it doesn't flatter your figure—you'd rather be uncomfortable or self-conscious than be left out of the fashion scene. Choosing to wear clothes that don't look good on you might be your way of saying you just can't stand the thought of being different from your friends. And you're right, it IS difficult to be different. But wearing clothes that don't look good on you will not help you to fit in. In fact, doing so may just make you stand out even more.

> **Terrific Teen Tip:** When Jade (age 15) feels like the latest clothing style doesn't fit her body, she doesn't buy it. Instead she looks for the "in" accessories and gets those instead. Shoes, pocketbooks, scarves, earrings, and other accessories go a long way towards making her feel in style, without having to be uncomfortable.

Here are a few more ideas to help you in a fashion slump. If the latest fashion doesn't flatter your figure, but you feel strongly that you need to fit in, look for clothes that are similar to the "in" style, but better for your body. For example, you may not look good in a skimpy sundress, but you may look beautiful in a dress that covers your body more fully, but is the same type of fabric or print. This may not always work because you can't always find equivalents, but often you will be successful. And when you do look good in the fashion of the moment, make the most of it and really enjoy yourself. That way you won't feel as deprived the next time you don't look great in the latest style.

Another way to resolve the fashion dilemma is to go in a different direction all together. Find a flattering style that makes a unique or unusual statement. Create your own, signature "look" that is all about you. Choose colors, fabrics, and accessories that show your own personal flare. You'll have no need for the latest fashion because your own fashion identity will be strong enough to carry you through.

Now you have a good idea about the social and media pressures that can really affect the way you feel about your body and interfere with your plans to become healthier and lose weight. No one (not friends, your family or the media) should take away your decision to gain control over your life and change your body. You now have some good tools to make changes in your outlook and your life. You're a step closer to really making those changes and becoming healthier.

So what's next? In Chapter 5, we'll make sure low self-esteem, depression, and other bad feelings don't get in the way of you becoming healthier and happier.

How Feelings Control
Your Eating

Do You Really Like Yourself?

For many girls responding to this question with a loud, confident YES isn't so simple. I speak with girls every day who tell me that they are unhappy with their bodies and it makes them feel upset or discouraged. But, I bet you'll be surprised when I tell you that it often works in the opposite way too: the sad or negative feelings come first and then the struggles with weight. In fact, if you felt better about yourself, you might feel better about your body. Even more importantly, if you felt better about yourself, you'd have the energy and motivation to work toward having a healthier body.

Now, let's take it one step further. What happens if you feel really bad about yourself most or all of the time? This is called "low self-esteem" or "low self-worth" and it affects many girls, often without them even realizing it. If you have low self-esteem, you might think of yourself in some of the following ways:

I hate myself
I'm unpopular
I'm ugly
I'm dumb
I'm an idiot
I'll never be good at anything
I'm a loser

You may find it interesting to know that many girls (and women) who struggle with their weight have low self-esteem. Low self-esteem is very often the cause of weight gain as well as one of the reasons for the ongoing struggle to lose weight.

Now, you're probably thinking *"but if I looked better, my self-esteem would improve, so all I need to do is lose weight and I'll feel great."* And you might be right, because it is possible that once you're looking better you will feel better. However, don't forget that if you don't like or value yourself, it will be difficult to find the strength or make the effort necessary to be able to change your weight or shape and become healthier and happier with how you look. After all, if you think of yourself as unlikable, hopeless, unpopular, ugly, or dumb, *you may not think you're worth the effort.* You might be thinking: *"Why should I waste my time trying to improve someone like me, who is so unlikable?"*

It's even possible that, aside from puberty and genetics (the healthy reasons for some weight gain), you may have gained extra weight BECAUSE you have low self-esteem.

When Too Little Self-Worth Means Too Much Food

Joelle (age 16) came to see me after her doctor told her she was more than sixty pounds overweight. She felt that there was no point in losing weight because it wouldn't change her life. Here's what Joelle told me:

82

"I look in the mirror every day and think I'm a fat slob. I can't imagine anyone liking me. And it's not only because I'm overweight. No one has ever liked me. In kindergarten they made fun of my name, in first grade they called me weird, in second grade they said I was a baby, and each year it got worse. I think kids still talk about me behind my back. I'm a loser. So, what's the point of trying to be healthier? At least I get some enjoyment out of eating. It's like I can make my mouth and stomach feel good, even when I can't make any other part of myself feel good.**"**

Joelle and I talked many times after that day. She eventually realized that the size of her body wasn't the only thing making her miserable. Rather, her bad feelings about her whole self had caused her to turn to food for comfort. She tried to make herself happy, and to hide bad feelings about herself. She had been unhappy most of her life because she'd been teased and felt lonely. Food became the one thing she could always count on not to let her down. Unfortunately, she gained a lot of weight while using food to soothe herself.

Not Me, Really!

Of course, not every overweight girl has low self-esteem, but since these feelings are sad, and painful, you may not want to admit that you have low self-esteem. Some girls believe that if they *act as if* they feel good about themselves, then people will think that they really do. They even pretend to themselves that everything is okay. This is called "denial." (I have to slip in a psychological term once in a while!)

Sometimes denial can help you. If you project a positive self-image, people will respond to it positively, and you may actually really begin to feel better. As you feel better, you become even more self-confident and so on. However, it doesn't always work this way.

Many girls act in an overly confident, pushy, and arrogant manner as a way to cover up their bad feelings. To other people, a girl who behaves like this will seem conceited, snobby or judgmental. In reality, she is usually hiding some very insecure feelings about herself.

Hiding low self-esteem in this way isn't only about being overweight. It's important to recognize that when you (or someone else) act like this, *there's a good chance the behavior is covering up feelings of low self-worth.* When people are truly self-confident and secure, they don't need to prove it to themselves or others.

How Do I Know for Sure?

To help you learn whether your self-esteem is rockin' or rocky, I've developed the following quiz (don't forget to use separate paper if it's not your book). For each scenario, find the response that comes closest to the way you think. If any one of these has never happened to you, do your best to imagine how you'd respond. The key here is to *be honest*. If you give the "correct," rather than the honest response, you will only be fooling yourself. Remember, finding the power to change must begin with honesty.

Enough Self Love Can Be Tough

1. During a heated discussion someone voices a strong disagreement with your point of view. In response you:

   a. Say "you're wrong," "that's dumb," "you don't make sense," "you know I'm right." You may yell, become angry, or voice your opinion even louder, without acknowledging the other person's point of view.

   b. Immediately back down from your position—either you

don't want conflict, or you begin to doubt your own opinion.

c. Ask the other person to explain herself fully, think about her point of view and then decide whether a compromise is in order.

2. You borrow your friend's favorite sweater without asking and get a stain on it. Your first response is to:

a. 'Fess up, apologize, immediately, offering to pay for the cleaning or replacement.

b. Convince yourself it wasn't your fault; if she didn't want you to wear it, she shouldn't have left it there.

c. Tell yourself "I'm such an idiot, I'm always messing up. I'm so pathetic."

3. You overhear your friends talking about the weekend but no one has mentioned the plans to you yet. You're thinking:

a. "It must be an oversight, I'll go over and ask them what's up for the weekend."

b. "Maybe they don't want to include me—I wonder what I did wrong?"

c. "Who needs them anyway, there are tons of people I can hang out with!"

4. Your boss compliments your hard work. You respond with:

a. "Thanks, I've been working really hard."

b. "Oh, it was nothing, anyone could've done it."

c. "Of course I did well, I'm awesome!"

5. Your best friend doesn't like your outfit. You:

a. Tell her she doesn't know what she's talking about.

b. Thank her for caring, consider whether you agree with her, and then decide if you should change your outfit.

c. Immediately change—you would never wear anything that someone else doesn't like.

6. You just found out that the guy you adore has started dating someone else. Of course you're disappointed so you tell yourself:

   a. It was inevitable because you're doomed to never have a boyfriend.
   b. He's an idiot and plot ways to embarrass him.
   c. Perhaps you're just not his type and then keep your eye open for a new guy.

7. Your mom won't let you go to a party with all your friends. Your friends think you should lie to your mom and go. You hate lying, but you're afraid that they'll think you're a wimp. You decide to:

   a. Tell your friends you can't make it—you'd rather miss the party than change your "no lying policy."
   b. Go with the lie—your mom will never know the difference.
   c. Say you'll do it, then, last minute pretend you're sick—you won't lie to your mom, but you can't face being thought of as a wimp.

8. It's Saturday night and you're at the movies with your parents. You run into a group of kids from school and your first reaction is to:

   a. Hide behind your popcorn—they'll think you're a loser for being out with your folks.
   b. Say hello—who cares what other people think.
   c. Roll your eyes and whisper, "they dragged me here, I can't wait for it to be over."

9. Tryouts just ended and you found out that you didn't make the cut. You:

   a. Cry, become depressed, and have trouble getting motivated for several days afterwards, thinking you're a failure.
   b. Are disappointed but resolve to find out what went wrong and try harder next time.
   c. Blame it on the judges—they were playing favorites.

10. Your boyfriend dumped you for another girl. She dumped him and now he wants to get back with you. You decide to:

    a. Get back with him and then dump *him* so he'll know how it feels.

    b. Tell him "no thanks." You can do better than him, and even if you can't right now, it's not worth degrading yourself.

    c. Gratefully get back together with him—any boyfriend is better than being alone.

11. Which of the following group of words most closely fits how you think about yourself?

    a. curious, a leader, confident, open-minded, sometimes wrong

    b. wishy-washy, a follower, usually wrong, negative, unsure

    c. strong-minded, self-assured, the boss, never wrong, a winner

12. Which of the following describes how you would deal with being yelled at for something you didn't do?

    a. Panic, cry, and immediately apologize.

    b. Yell back, deny responsibility, and tell the other person it's their fault.

    c. Calmly ask the other person to stop yelling, explain why the accusation is incorrect, and then request an apology.

Scoring:

1. a = 2, b = 0, c = 1   2. a = 1, b = 2, c = 0   3. a = 1, b = 0, c = 2
4. a = 1, b = 0, c = 2   5. a = 2, b = 1, c = 0   6. a = 0, b = 2, c = 1
7. a = 1, b = 2, c = 0   8. a = 0, b = 1, c = 2   9. a = 0, b = 1, c = 2
10. a = 2, b = 1, c = 0   11. a = 1, b = 0, c = 2   12. a = 0, b = 2, c = 1

Now, add up your scores and find your category:

	Answer	Score		Answer	Score	
1.			7.			
2.			8.			
3.			9.			
4.			10			
5.			11.			
6.			12.			TOTAL
			+		=	

Too Little Self Love (0–8 points)

It looks like you focus on the negative parts of yourself. The lower your score, the more your self-esteem is suffering. You find it difficult to accept a compliment and you typically give someone or something else the credit for your achievements. You seem to have given up on yourself, perhaps accepting that it's okay for people to treat you badly, or taking blame for things you may not have done. You also find it hard to stand up for what you believe in. Maybe you're afraid that if you don't agree with others, they won't like you.

It's a good bet that your low self-esteem is getting in the way of you becoming healthier. You may not yet feel good about your body, but you're reading *Dr. Susan's Girls-Only Weight Loss Guide*, which is the first step toward making positive, healthy changes. BUT, before you can begin to change your body, you need to like yourself! You're worth the hard work, the commitment, and the motivation it will take to become healthier.

There are many ways to feel better about yourself and you will find them throughout this book. In fact, at the end of this section you will find a list of thirty ways to begin feeling good about yourself. But, you should start right now by making your own list of at least five things that you love to do (except eating!). Perhaps it's as simple as reading a chapter in your favorite book, taking a bubble bath, talking to your best friend on the phone, or visiting your grandma. Then, starting today, try to do at least one of these things each day, even if it's just for five minutes. By giving yourself something you love, you will be taking the first step to valuing and appreciating yourself.

A Beautiful Balance (9–15)

Congratulations! You've been working hard to make sure that you feel good about yourself and that's something to be proud of. Being a girl is not always easy. From the physical changes to the emotional curves to the social complications, life is always a challenge. But through it all you've managed to remember that no matter what happens it's important to be true to yourself and to your values. Check out the other two sections anyway, to be sure that you aren't dipping into either one. But keep in mind that your struggles to become healthier and happier with how you look are probably more about other things we discuss in the book. So hang on to your good feelings and keep reading!

Hiding from Yourself (16–24)

You're in that tough area that we've called "denial." Your super-confident exterior is probably hiding a less secure inner self (take a minute to reread the section titled *"Not Me, Really"*). Underneath your tough exterior you're probably nervous that being wrong or unsure means you're stupid or imperfect. You like to come across as super-confident, and always in charge. This façade keeps your secret well hidden—if people think you're tough and confident, they won't realize that underneath, you're vulnerable and unsure of yourself. You may have even convinced yourself that everything is okay. But now it's time to realize that you will have to make changes in order to be emotionally healthier and feel truly happy. You see, if you can't admit to negative parts of yourself, you will also struggle to acknowledge that you need to make changes in your eating and exercise in order to become physically healthier and to feel better.

But if you follow the following eight steps you will come closer to finding the real you. It may take a long time to complete all the steps. But you'll find that it's worth it. Once you're strong enough to see that, like all of us, you have faults, you will be able to work on changing them so that you can feel *truly* good about yourself.

8 Steps to Finding the REAL You

1. Find a quiet time and comfortable place to begin thinking. Grab some paper and a pen.

2. Make a list of words describing how you think other people see you. These will probably be words like confident, self-assured, happy, knowledgeable, smart, and so on.

3. Now make a list of how you *really* secretly feel about yourself. Some words may be the same, but most will probably be different. Don't be surprised if these aren't how you want people to see you. You might want to work on this list for a few days. Don't go on to the next step until you've uncovered all the parts of yourself that you don't show to others.

4. Find an adult with whom you can talk. Explain to her or him that there are two sides to you—a public side and a private side. Talk about how you can begin to bring the two parts of you together into one person.

5. Now, read the results for the quiz category Too Little Love, because you're likely to find that once you acknowledge your secret side, many of your feelings will fit in this category. The overly confident image you're showing is most likely covering up sad, bad feelings about yourself.

6. Now, check out The Top 30 Ways to Value Yourself, coming up next.

7. You may start to feel confused, depressed or angry as you go through these steps. It's normal to have bad feelings when you're struggling with emotional conflict. BUT, *don't keep the feelings to yourself!!!!* Talk to an adult or friend so that you don't have to struggle alone.

8. Think about whether your bad feelings about your body are really tied up with your secret self. Maybe it's hard to acknowledge that you're unhappy with your body; or maybe it's easier to continue struggling with your body than it is to focus on the secret feelings that would upset you even more.

Everyone Needs a Boost Once in a While!

No matter what your score on the quiz, just about every girl (and woman) can benefit from a reminder that she is valuable and important. Life can be so hectic sometimes, and we can get so caught up in all the negatives that we need help developing or holding onto a positive outlook. But Dr. Susan is here to help! Below is a list of thirty ideas that are a great way to get you going. Start with any one of them right now, and don't stop until you've tried them all. It may take a few weeks, a few months or even years. But don't give up because you deserve to be loved, especially by yourself. After you try out some of these ideas you may come up with others. If you have any terrific ways to boost self-esteem, you can email them to me at DrSusan@girlsonlyweightloss.com.

The Top 30 Ways to Value Yourself

1. Look at yourself in the mirror and smile at your reflection.

2. Get all your homework done early, then take a long bath, watch a great movie, or do something else you love.

3. Make a list of the things you like about yourself (even if it starts out with only one item)—each week add one thing to the list. Spend two minutes (time it on your alarm clock) before getting out of bed each morning thinking about your list. Also, spend two minutes in bed each night thinking about your list.

4. When someone compliments you say "thank you," smile, and then don't say another word.

5. Give away any clothes or shoes that aren't comfortable or that you don't like on yourself.

6. Speak loudly and with confidence—even if you have to fake it.

7. Don't focus on the negatives—if you make a mistake, tell yourself "no one's perfect" and move on.

8. Stand up for what you really believe in—your opinion is as valid as anyone else's.

9. Recognize that bad things sometimes happen to everyone, not just you.

10. Realize that you often have more control than you think—whether you study, practice, concentrate or try can affect how successful you will be.

11. Make a decision to give something your all—study for a test, practice for a tennis tournament, learn to knit. It doesn't matter what you pick, just give it your maximum effort.

12. Confront someone who has hurt your feelings. Don't fight, but tell them how you feel.

13. Don't put yourself down—even if everyone else is saying negative things about themselves.

14. Once in a while, buy yourself something that really makes you feel good about yourself.

15. Start a journal. No matter how bad you're feeling, at the beginning of each entry write something positive about yourself.

16. Stop wishing you were someone else or that you looked like someone other than you. Instead, start to think about how to make yourself happier inside your own body.

17. Ask for help when you need it—it doesn't matter whether it's for something very small or very big.

18. Find an adult who you can trust with your feelings (some ideas are: parent, aunt, grandmother, teacher, school counselor, doctor, friend's parent, religious leader, youth group leader). When you need to talk, GO TO THIS ADULT and actually talk.

19. Don't get together (or back together) with a guy who you don't really like, and don't get together (or back together) with a guy who doesn't treat you with respect and care.

20. If someone teases you or puts you down, tell yourself it's not about you: insecure people are sometimes mean to others to make themselves feel better. Without a victim, a bully would have to face her own fears, so don't let yourself be the victim (but don't be a bully either).

21. Start each day with a specific goal for that day that reflects good self-worth. Work toward achieving it (some ideas: raise your hand in class, smile at your crush, assert your opinion, change your hairstyle, speak a bit louder, don't put yourself down).

22. Realize that your self-worth has nothing to do with your successes or failures—getting an "A" on a test doesn't make you a better person and failing to lose 10 pounds doesn't make you a worse person.

23. Don't do anything you know you shouldn't do or that you don't want to do (e.g., sex, smoking, drinking, drugs, skipping class, lying to your parents, deceiving your friends) just because other people are doing it. When you go against your gut feeling to be cool or to fit in, it will only backfire and make you feel awful about yourself.

24. Ask someone you love for a hug—you deserve one and so do they.

25. Don't focus on small negatives—a pimple, bad haircut, a bad grade on a test—these things will be over in a few days or weeks. They happen to everyone and are never as bad as they seem that minute.

26. Stop "if-then'ing" yourself. For example, if I lose 20 pounds then I'll be happy.

27. Spend time only with people who treat you well. Ditch those that don't value your friendship.

28. Start a collection of warm and wonderful things that people have given you—birthday cards, thank-you notes, photos, emails—that you can pull out and look at when you're feeling low.

29. Reach out to long distance friends. Sometimes far away friends can make you feel really valued because they miss you. Emails, phone calls or letters to and from these friends can remind you how special you are.

30. Find something you're good at—a sport, a craft, babysitting, volunteering, a job, a subject in school—and do that thing a lot!

My Life Makes Me Eat!

Kelly (age 15), one of the girls in my Advisory Group, was three months old when her parents divorced. For about six years, her dad wasn't really in her life. When he returned it was complicated at first, but eventually they developed a strong, loving relationship.

I first worked with Kelly when she was four to help her get through some of her tough early years. She had struggled with separations from her mom and other people—understandable considering she'd lost a family unit and her dad for a long time. Once Kelly became secure and happy, we said good-bye and I didn't see her again for several years.

When Kelly was fourteen, her mom called to say that Kelly wanted to come back to see me. She had gained a lot of weight and both Kelly and her pediatrician were unhappy with the way she looked. When I met with Kelly again, for the first time as a teenager, this is what she told me:

> **"I** know I'm stuffing myself with food as a way to stuff down my feelings. It's hard being a teenager and there are still lots of things going on in my family. Also, it's a bit weird to give up being a little girl and become a teenager. It's sort of like a separation from my mom again, the way I used to be afraid of separating from her when I was younger.**"**

Do You Eat Your Feelings Away?

For some girls, the struggle with eating is connected to low self-esteem and many other girls, like Kelly, eat for reasons that have everything to do with their feelings. They eat to avoid feeling depressed, to reduce anxiety, when they're angry, or when they're happy.

I asked fifty girls if they ever connect food and feelings. I was amazed to find that forty-six of the fifty girls said YES! Here are twelve of the answers that show us the most common ways in which teenage girls connect food and feelings:

1. Linda (age 17): After I fight with my boyfriend, I always eat cookies. And then afterwards I'm angry with myself for letting him get to me like that!

2. Ada (age 12): When I'm depressed, like after my parents got divorced, or my brother left for college, I make myself oatmeal and hot chocolate—it makes me feel better.

3. Devon (age 18): When I feel like I've accomplished something I always give myself a "junk food treat." Last week I finished a huge essay for my economics class so I celebrated with a bag of caramel popcorn.

4. Marie (age 15): When I'm really happy, like at a party, I eat a lot. But afterwards I always feel really guilty.

5. Gloria (age 16): I eat when I'm bored. It's something to do, rather than just sitting around.

6. Sophie (age 14): When I'm sad, I love to eat peanut butter on toast—it reminds me of when I was little—my mom used to give it to me when I was upset.

7. Althea (age 18): When I'm worried I eat. Some people can't eat when they're worried—I wish that was my problem!

8. Kathleen (age 14): When I was younger, my grandma would get angry if I didn't eat all my food. She would say there are starving children who would be grateful for my leftovers. So now I feel guilty if I don't eat everything on the plate.

9. Tameka (age 16): I find myself eating when I'm nervous, like before a piano recital. I usually eat saltine crackers or pretzels because they won't mess my dress.

10. Kristy (age 15): My friends and I always get pizza after a big test—we're so relieved it's over.

11. Molly (age 13): My sister eats constantly and she's thin. I'm not thin and it upsets me that I have to watch what I eat and she doesn't. So I eat a lot anyway, especially when I'm most aggravated with her being thin.

12. Cecelia (age 17): Being angry makes me want to eat and then if I can't find exactly what I want (Rocky Road ice cream) I get even angrier. And if I find out that someone else just finished the Rocky Road ice cream (my roommate!), well . . . you can just imagine!

The Food-Mood Connection

So, do you eat your feelings away? I've come up with a great way to figure it out so try this food-mood exercise for one week (that's seven whole days) to discover how much your eating and emotions are interconnected.

Dr. Susan's Food-Mood Experiment

Get a notebook and divide the first page into three columns. Now, at the top of the first column write "food," at the top of the second column write "mood," and at the top of the third column write "effect."

For the next seven days, take the notebook everywhere and write what you eat in the first column (using extra pages as you need them). In the middle column write how you feel before you eat that food. You should also note whether you were actually hungry before you began eating. In the third column, write down how you feel after you eat the food. At the end of each day your chart should look something like this one:

My Food-Mood Chart

Food	Mood	Effect
MONDAY breakfast—frosted flakes with milk, a diet soda	A little hungry, tired, don't want to go to school	About the same, not so hungry
11a.m.—potato chips, iced tea	Aggravated—Tony was talking to Maggie, he just ignores me, not hungry at all	Guilty and fat—I should've had some fruit, no wonder Tony doesn't pay attention to me
12:30—lunch—two slices of pizza with extra cheese, frozen yogurt, diet soda	Pretty good mood—we left school for lunch, I was hungry but could've been okay with one slice, but everyone was having two, so what if I did too!	Kind of sluggish, don't feel like going back for p.m. classes

3:45—cheeseburger, diet soda, medium fries	Angry!!!!! I found out I got a C+ on my Chemistry midterm, I don't think I'm that hungry, but who cares I'm eating it anyway	Still angry!!!! But at least I ate what I wanted—I'll probably feel guilty later, always do
6:30—dinner—mom's late from work again, it's take-out fried chicken	Nervous to tell her about the C+, I'm eating a lot, I can tell, always eat when I'm nervous	I'm full, ate too much but I told her about the test and she wasn't really upset, whew!
9:20—four cookies and a bowl of cheese puffs	Tired, but still have tons of homework to do, this snack will keep me going	Gives me a bit of energy, but now I'm obsessing about wanting more, instead of finishing my work, but I'm not going back down to the kitchen
9:40—five more cookies	Ok, ok, so I couldn't hold off, but now I'm done	I'm trying not to think about it, today was a bad eating day—I'll have more control tomorrow (I think I said that yesterday)

It's possible that being aware of your eating while doing this exercise will affect your eating habits. Doing it for at least a week will give you enough time to become accustomed to the fact that you're taking notes so that hopefully your eating behavior will return to normal after the first couple of days. A full week will also give you an opportunity to experience many different emotions.

Here is a list of possible feelings for you to consider as you're working on your journal. Feel free to add any that apply to you:

happy	moody	joyful
sad	tired	depressed
angry	relieved	lazy
disappointed	worried	melancholy
nervous	anxious	optimistic
excited	bored	tense

Note: This is **not** a calorie-counting exercise so there is no reason to keep track of the amounts of food you eat.

Proving the Patterns

At the end of the week, take a look at your journal. You will notice patterns connecting how you feel with how and what you eat, and you'll also notice how you felt after eating. On a new page in your journal, write down your list of patterns. Here's an example to help you. Your list may be similar or very different from the sample one below.

My List of Eating Patterns

* I eat a whole bag of chips or pretzels when I'm bored. Afterwards I feel bad and promise myself I won't do it again—I always do it again.

* I eat chocolate when I'm hanging out at Cathy's house. I feel good afterwards because Cathy and I love doing everything together.

* Liz eats three slices of pizza but she's still so skinny. I'm really overweight but if she can eat three slices, I will too. I'm jealous before I eat and guilty afterwards.

* I eat soft chocolate-chip cookies while I'm doing math homework. I hate math so I dread doing the work, and I love the cookies so it makes the homework bearable. After I finish, I always tell myself that the extra calories were worth it to get my math done. I think I deserve those cookies, I just wish I could stop at one or two instead of a whole package.

* The day after I begin a diet, I start to feel like I'm going to lose control if I eat one wrong thing. Usually by day three, I've given up on the diet and I'm eating even more than I was before. I feel guilty, but I keep eating.

* I'm starving when I get home from classes and I want something quick so I have a bowl of cereal. I feel better afterwards—I

don't see any emotional connection here, I guess I'm just hungry after school. I wish all my eating was this simple!

Feel It, Don't Fake It with Food

After you've figured out how eating helps you cope with, or express, your feelings, and how eating makes you feel, you're ready for the next step. This is the hardest, but most important part of the exercise.

Your goal is to learn how to deal with your feelings without relying on food. You will need to come up with *different* ways to experience your feelings that don't include eating. Of course, it is important to eat when you're hungry, and even to eat just because something tastes good. But eating as a response to emotions is not good for you. It probably makes you eat more than your body needs and it allows you to avoid dealing directly with your feelings.

Learning to choose other ways to express your feelings is an excellent step toward feeling healthier and happier with your body. Coming up next you will see some great ways (that don't include eating) to deal with different emotions. You will probably find that you have more than one situation or emotion that triggers emotional eating, so you'll be able to benefit from several of the tips below. But don't stop there! Come up with your own ideas for dealing with your feelings in non-eating ways. Your own ideas will not only fit your specific needs, but you will also be taking an active step towards helping yourself feel better. I'd love to hear your ideas, so email them to me at DrSusan@girlsonlyweightloss.com.

Dr Susan's Terrific Tips

✳ Boredom: Rather than eating when you're bored, read or do a crossword puzzle instead. Stay away from the TV, because all the food commercials and the association between watching TV and eating will just make you want to eat more. With just a little effort, you don't have to let eating be the only answer to boredom.

❋ **Sadness:** Being sad makes many girls want to treat themselves with sweets. But instead, do yourself a favor and treat yourself in other ways—put on your favorite outfit, call your best friend or take a bubble-bath (my ultimate favorite!)—it helps just as much.

❋ **Mindless eating:** For lots of girls, one of the biggest triggers for mindless eating is while hanging out with friends. But you will come to realize that although eating is *part* of the fun, being with your friends is what's really important. A great way to have both is to eat a bit so you don't feel left out and then, instead of concentrating on the food, you should focus on the conversation instead.

❋ **Performance anxiety:** Sometimes people eat when they're anxious about how they will do on a test, performance or presentation because they feel eating calms and distracts them. But there are better ways to cope with this feeling. You need to make sure you're as prepared as possible for the presentation. For example, instead of eating, go over your notes beforehand. Dealing with the things that *really* making you anxious, works much better than being distracted by food.

❋ **Worrying:** It's not unusual for people to eat when they're worried—perhaps you're waiting to hear about college acceptances or about a job interview—but, in reality it doesn't make you any less worried. What's more, eating won't really get your worries answered any faster. Instead, spend some time thinking about what you will do if your worries come true. You may not like to think about this, but when you do, you will discover that life is full of alternative choices for approaching even the most negative situations.

❋ **Feeling criticized:** When girls feel criticized (by their mom, friend, teacher, or boyfriend, just to name a few), they sometimes turn to eating to try and help themselves feel better. But, really, eating like this just makes you gain more weight, so it's important to learn other ways to cope with criticism from others. Try to remain open-minded about the criticism, but even if you're angry, talk to someone, go for a jog, or write down your feelings in a journal. Do whatever you can to face your feelings without eating. It's not easy, but it's what you have to do. Be determined to take responsibility for what you put in my body.

✳ Tiredness: Some girls eat when they're tired because they think it will give them energy. If you're tired *because* you're hungry, then eating is a good solution. But if you're tired because you haven't had enough sleep, then you should take a nap. If you're dragging and need to shake yourself into alertness, try blasting great music to get you going. These solutions will stop you from eating for the wrong reasons, and also take care of your tiredness.

Easy Does It

Confronting your emotional eating may seem like a huge task. I suggest that you NOT try to change everything at once. Once you've defined your personal triggers for eating, you can start by choosing one trigger situation to work on at a time. Once you've mastered it, go back to the list and pick another one. And since, it can be very difficult to recognize all the ways you've allowed food to make you happier, reduce anxiety, calm rage, and fill you up emotionally, it could take months (or even longer) to learn how to eat only for hunger and taste instead of for feelings.

Terrific Teen Tip: Carly (age 14) decided to pick the trigger situation that was easiest for her (eating when she was tired) rather than the most difficult (eating when she was upset). She found it quite easy to stop eating when she was tired, and this gave her the confidence to challenge herself to stop eating in other emotional situations. She continued from the easiest trigger to the most difficult ones until she had mastered them all. It took her about two years, but she says her healthy body was worth every challenge!

More Power to You

Over time, you will collect many different ways to manage your feelings that don't include eating. Perhaps you will do more: explaining, writing, crying, walking, reading, insisting, drawing, running, painting, sharing, singing, playing, debating, pacing, thinking, creating, dancing, and/or studying. You will become a stronger, more resilient, more in control, more powerful, and clearer thinking person. You will understand and respect your feelings more fully. Food will become nourishment for your *body*, not a substitute for these healthier pursuits that will truly make you happy.

Really Bad Feelings

If you find it really difficult to cope with your feelings, or if you're going through an especially difficult time in your life, you may need to reach out for extra help beyond this book. Some girls feel very anxious, lonely, depressed or even like they want to die or kill themselves—they may not even know why. Other girls have experienced, or are going through traumatic life events like parents divorcing, or someone they love dying. Maybe they have been physically or emotionally hurt in some way. Or perhaps they are or have been bullied or teased. If you have had or are having any of these experiences, it is very important for you to ask for help in order to cope. Your parents, school counselor, medical doctor, religious leader or a professional therapist will be able to get the help you need, so don't keep these things a secret. You will also find some resources in Appendix 2.

Six

Predictable Family Patterns

"(Abigail, age 15) My parents are very overweight and constantly try to "get skinny." I admire them for trying but they never really get there. My mom's goal is to look like she did when she was eighteen—even I know that's nuts! The diets only last a few days and then it's back to greasy takeout and cookies. I try the diets too, but I think I'm getting larger. I wish I could figure out how to lose the weight for good!**"**

For many girls the struggle with food and weight begins in their families. Some parents don't even realize they are communicating unhealthy eating patterns and ideas to their children. For example, Abigail's parents are trying to lose weight. But it's clear to Abigail that the roller-coaster dieting and "throw in the towel" fast food eating between diets, is not healthy. Abigail also realizes that it's unrealistic for her mom to even try to look the way she did at eighteen (good for her!). And she knows how difficult it is to eat in a healthy way in her own home.

Even with all this knowledge, Abigail may not understand the enormous impact of having spent most of her life observing her parents dieting inconsistently, rarely exercising, and swinging between gaining and losing weight. This is the pattern in her family. It is the way she has learned to approach food and exercise since she was very young, and it may be difficult to change it.

For some girls, like Abigail, the pattern develops just by watching their parents, or by living the same way as their parents. For other girls, unhealthy patterns develop because of things that are said to them. For example, Mae's (age 14) mother frequently told Mae that girls are supposed to diet so they will look their best. When a strong message is communicated in this way, especially by a parent, it can be difficult to reject the message, even if it is really unhealthy. As you can imagine the message Mae received from her mother about dieting made it very difficult for Mae to break a dieting pattern that was not helping her become healthier. Sometimes your parents' (or even other family members') influences can make it tough for you to make your own choices. You may fear that they will disapprove, reject you, or be critical of you. This can be one of the biggest hurdles to overcome when you're trying to break unhealthy patterns and begin to live a healthier lifestyle.

But your fears may be unfounded. In fact, in many cases your family will be very supportive of changes you want to make—they may even make them with you. However, if your family does not approve of or support you, this is no reason to give up. It is time for you to understand that not every communication you receive from your mom, dad or other adult is healthy for you. You are now old enough to make good choices for your life, regardless of whether your parents support you. It may be a bit more difficult without their support, but it is not an excuse to give up.

Facing Your Family's Food Flaws

This chapter is unusual because it will teach things that you've probably never seen in any diet you've tried. You will learn to understand how overeating may be a part of a pattern created by your family. All families have relationships with food. But, like Abigail's family, many develop unhealthy patterns that then cause you (and other members) to become overweight. In order to make lifelong, healthy changes, it is important to understand these patterns, recognize how they are contributing to you being overweight, and then break away from them. You might not be able to change your parents or other family members, but you will be able to gain control of your own body and health. Although it may be difficult at times, *it is important for you to make healthy choices for yourself regardless of the way members of your family treat their bodies or how they feel about yours.*

We will look at six patterns—Clean Your Plate, Forbidden Foods, Snacking is Sweeter, Fast Living—Fast Food, Dieting and Denying, and Sibling Stress. You will learn how, without even realizing it, your parents and even your grandparents may negatively influence your eating and relationship with food.

Struggles with eating and being overweight can actually be passed down from parents to their children for many generations and for lots of different reasons. Your parents' attitudes towards food and eating were probably influenced by the attitudes of their parents (as well as by culture or religion). Talk to your parents (and even your grandparents) about food and eating in their families growing up. If you find it hard to explain why you're doing this, let them read this chapter.

Here are some ideas for questions to ask your parents and grandparents to help you understand patterns in your family:

1. When you were a child did you have enough food to eat?

2. Did your parents make you finish all your food, or did they encourage you to stop eating when you were full?

3. Did you get enough "snack food" or did you feel deprived compared to other kids?

4. Did your mom or dad struggle with their weight? Did they talk about dieting often?

5. Did your mom or dad focus too much on your eating? Were they critical of your body?

6. Did you feel happy with your body growing up?

7. Was food a big part of socializing in your family growing up?

8. Was your mom/dad a good cook?

You can also try to figure out the patterns by watching the way people in your family speak about food and eating, and by how they eat.

You may find that your family fits into more than one category. If so, you will be able to benefit from the tips and suggestions in each area that you recognize as problematic for you. For example, if your family fits the Clean Your Plate pattern, you will learn how to listen to your body's hunger cues, rather than simply eating what's in front of you. If, at the same time, your family fits the Fast Living—Fast Food or Snacking is Sweeter, categories, you will also learn how to make changes in your lifestyle so that you are eating more healthily, regardless of whether other people in your family make any changes.

Even if your parents haven't passed down unhealthy eating patterns, it is still likely that you've developed some of your own, such as eating secretly, eating when you're not hungry, or living a fast-food lifestyle. So even without a family pattern, you will benefit from the many suggestions and ideas we will discuss.

Whether the patterns began with your parents or with you, there is probably arguing, tension or fighting about your eating (and exercise) habits. This is especially true if your parents disapprove of your choices or if they don't struggle with their weight. So we'll look at different ways to calm things down in your family, alleviate the stress around food, and stop the fighting about your body.

But *you don't have to make all the changes at once.* If you do it a little at a time, you will have a much greater chance of success. So, here we go—keep yourself tuned in for patterns you may recognize.

Pattern #1: Clean Your Plate

"Theresa (age 15): I feel like I've been a "large" girl my whole life and I really hate it! I have tried to watch my weight many, many times since I was about thirteen, but every time I tried there seemed to be another huge plate of food in front of me. Also, my mother always said that growing children have to eat. I was growing alright—but OUT, not up! Now I've finally decided to help myself look and feel better. A friend told me that Dr. Susan had really helped her so I'm hoping she'll help me too."

I suggested that it may help Theresa if she tried to uncover the eating patterns in her family, so she spoke to her parents and grandparents about how they grew up. She found out that her mother's parents (Theresa's grandparents) were both poor as children. They rarely had enough to eat, and were often hungry. Eventually they married and then had a successful dry cleaning business. So by the time they had children (Theresa's mom and uncle) they were no longer poor. Since they remembered how awful it felt to be truly hungry, they made sure there was lots of food in the house. And because they didn't ever want their children to experience real hunger, they pressured their children to eat even when they were full. Additionally, since food had been so precious to them as children, they couldn't stand to see it left on the plate. "Clean your plate" and "there are starving children who would love this dinner" were phrases commonly heard by Theresa's mom when she was a child. As a result, Theresa's mom grew up feeling that it was important to always feed your children a lot. She also believed that children should eat everything on the plate. You can guess what happened with Theresa: she grew up in a home with plenty of food, but she wasn't taught to stop eating when she was full. Theresa also felt guilty if she left food behind, so she always cleaned her plate, no matter how full her stomach felt.

I'm sure you can see the family pattern—Theresa's grandparents, who were truly deprived of food as children, needed to make sure this didn't happen with their children. By the time it came to Theresa, she felt she should eat even when she wasn't hungry because in this family, eating wasn't really about hunger. It was about not depriving your children.

So Theresa struggled a great deal with her weight because she typically ate much more than her body needed to be healthy. But even when Theresa was a kid and the doctor told her mom to help Theresa lose weight, her mom couldn't do it because she was afraid Theresa might get hungry. Theresa's mom was afraid that if she didn't keep feeding Theresa it meant that she might be a bad parent.

If you come from a "clean your plate" family, ask yourself these questions to try and uncover the truth:

* Does your parent ask you constantly if you're hungry?
* Is it just expected in your house that everyone will have at least seconds at each meal?
* Will your mom or dad become angry, upset, insulted or hurt if you don't eat everything on your plate?
* Is dieting considered a crime in your family?
* Is there always a meal or snack offered in your home long before you can even think about being really truly hungry?
* Are there always leftovers in the refrigerator because your mom or dad made way too much for dinner?

If you answered a resounding "yes" to at least some—and maybe all—of these questions, it is likely that you join Theresa in the Clean Your Plate club. When you eat without paying attention to your body's physical need for food you almost always will end up eating more than you need which, of course, will result in your body being larger than it should be.

Aha! Now I Understand!

Growing up in a family like this can exert some powerful influences over your eating habits. It is only now as an adult that Theresa has taken the time to realize she doesn't have to go along with her mom's need to feed. She's breaking away, making healthier eating choices and most importantly she realizes that food and love are two separate things. Eating smaller amounts of food doesn't mean she's deprived. She doesn't need to eat to feel loved by her mom and she doesn't need to eat everything her mom offers to make her mom feel she's a good parent.

The First Step

When she first started saying "no thank you" to her mom's offer for second or third helpings, her mom became upset or even angry because Theresa was "wasting" food. But Theresa understood her family pattern, so she explained to her mom that she couldn't keep eating just to finish the food. She learned that she needed to *pay attention to when she was really hungry* and stop eating when she was full. Luckily, Theresa's mom learned too and stopped forcing Theresa to eat. Both Theresa and her mom kept working at it until they'd broken the Clean Your Plate habit.

There are many girls who have a family pattern similar to Theresa's. If your family's approach to food has resulted in you eating beyond hunger or needing to "clean your plate," you will need to make some changes, just as Theresa did.

I know it can be tough to talk to your mom (or dad or grandparent) about making changes, but you really need to do your best to speak to them directly. If you're not sure what to say, write it out and even read it to them. However, if it is really too difficult to describe what you need, below is a "fill in the blank" letter you can rewrite (by hand or on the computer) and then give to your parents to help them understand the changes you'd like to make in your eating. Of course, you don't have to follow the letter exactly. You can use the ideas to come up with your own way of getting the point across to your parents. You can also give them this chapter to read.

Dear _____(Mom/Dad)

Lately I have been thinking about the eating patterns in our family. I realize now that our family has a "clean the plate" *approach to eating. Ever since I was young, I've always been taught to finish everything on the plate and sometimes even to eat more, even when I'm not hungry. I know that you only want the best for me and that you give me lots of food because you love me. But, I see now that eating when I'm not hungry is not helping me to have the healthiest body, and I'm not very happy about how my body looks and feels.*

I'd like to ask for your help to change my eating pattern. Please give me slightly smaller portions of food on my plate at meals. Next, don't offer me second or third helpings. You don't have to worry that I will be hungry. I promise that if I am hungry, I will ask for more. Also, please don't get angry with me if I don't finish everything on my plate because I need to learn to eat only when I am hungry, not because there is still food on the plate. I know this is different from the way we've always done things, but I would really appreciate your help and I'm sure it will help me to feel and look healthier.

Love _____(your name)

What if It Doesn't Work?

Your parents will likely appreciate the effort you are making to improve your health and to feel better about yourself. But it is possible that your parents may feel that you don't think they've been good parents or that you're blaming them for your unhappiness with your body. If your parents become angry or hurt by your request, you won't be able to get them to support the changes you want to make.

This is part of growing up—sometimes you have to rely only on yourself to become a healthier person—physically and even emotionally. This is true in all areas; it's not just about eating and it's not just about your body. Sometimes your parents can help you, and sometimes they can't. Ultimately, it is up to you to make sure you are happy and healthy.

Making the Changes

Regardless of parental support, you need to break free of eating auto-matically and begin paying attention to whether your body is hungry or not. If you can master the ability to eat when you're hungry and stop eating when you're satisfied, you will have come a long way toward having a healthier body and a healthy attitude toward eating. I spoke with many girls (including Theresa) who have accomplished this goal. Here are their excellent suggestions.

Heed Your Hunger

1. **Learn what real hunger feels like.** The next time you feel hungry, first have a drink of water because sometimes when you're thirsty your brain reads it as hunger. If the hunger pangs continue, you will know you are really hungry. Now, EAT SOMETHING!

   - The rule: When you are actually hungry, you should eat!

2. **Eat something that will satisfy your hunger.** Once you've discovered you are hungry EAT ENOUGH FOOD. Some-times when girls are unhappy with their bodies they feel guilty about eating, so when they're hungry they don't eat enough to satisfy their hunger. Your body needs enough food to be fueled with energy (we'll talk more about this in Chapters 7 and 8), so when you're hungry *eat without guilt*.

   - The rule: Eat enough real food.

3. **Try not to eat if you're not hungry.** Instead, wait a while before eating. You won't need to postpone eating indef-initely, only until you're really hungry. So, if your mom makes a fabulous dinner, and calls you to eat, first decide whether you're hungry. If you're not, wait until later. If

you're worried there will be none left, put aside a plate of food for yourself.

- **The rule:** If you're not hungry, don't eat, but don't skip meals!

4. **Eat slowly to give your stomach a chance to send the message to your brain that you're full.** If you eat quickly you might be on your second or third helping before your brain starts to register that you were stuffed ten minutes ago. If you've always "cleaned the plate," you've never needed to decide whether you are full. So now you will need to chew thoroughly, put the fork down between bites, eat one piece at a time and take small mouthfuls. Don't stop eating before you're satisfied, but don't keep going once you are.

- **The rule:** Eat slowly and pay attention to what your body is telling you.

5. **If you're offered another helping think about how your stomach feels.** If you're still hungry, have more food. Eat as much as you need to feel satisfied. But if your stomach is full after the first helping, don't feel bad about saying, "no thank you."

- **The rule:** Don't feel that you must eat more just because it's offered.

It may not be easy to heed your hunger, but it is an important achievement for anyone that wants a healthier body and a healthier relationship with food. It could take a while before you're able to achieve rules one through five, but you'll feel awesome once you get there!

Pattern #2: Forbidden Foods

"Jodi (age 16): I'm so fed up with dieting, dieting, dieting! My rolls of fat are a constant reminder that I shouldn't eat any of the foods I really want, like cookies or—my favorite—chocolate-covered malt balls. I try really hard, but once in a while I just go crazy for something sweet. Of course, then I overdo it totally. Is this self-control or a complete lack of control?"

Jodi has struggled with her weight since she was young. She has been called "fatty" and is always picked last for sports. When she came to see me, Jodi explained that she desperately wanted a healthier body, but she panicked at the thought of having to diet. I reminded Jodi that she should never "diet"! Diets almost always fail and dieting is not a healthy way for a girl (or a woman for that matter) to feel better about her body.

I suggested that Jodi study her family to see if she could find any eating patterns that interfered with her becoming healthier. So Jodi filled her journal with thoughts and observations about her family. She agreed to let me share a few entries:

Monday, February 18

Today I realized something important—we don't have any junk food in our house. NOTHING AT ALL. Why is that, I wonder?

Tuesday, February 19

I asked mom why we don't have junk food and she said because then I'd have even more weight problems than I do already. I'm not sure about that. We didn't have junk food when I was a little kid, but I still got fat somehow.

Thursday, February 20

I remember that when I was little, I would go to my neighbor's house whenever I could because she always had great cookies. I'd eat as many as possible before going home. I never told my mom about it. She would've been really mad.

Friday, February 21

I still sneak junk food whenever my mom isn't around. I take cookies or chips from the college cafeteria and eat them in my room while I do my homework. At friends' houses, I always eat tons of snack food. How come everyone else has junk food and we don't?

Saturday, February 22

My mom sneaks junk food, too! Is it okay to eat secretly? Will that make you thin? NO, NO, NO it will not. I wonder if my mom feels as guilty as I do about eating junk food? I guess she does because otherwise she wouldn't sneak it. I think it's the secret junk food eating that's making me fat! Wait 'til I tell Dr. Susan that I've found the pattern!!!

Are you wondering if you fit into the **Forbidden Foods** pattern? It's easy to figure it out, simply by asking yourself the following questions and thinking about your answers:

- ❀ Do you live in a home with no junk food?

- ❀ If there is some junk food in your home, will you eat it secretly in your room or when no one is looking?

- ❀ Do you notice that your mother or father sometime sneak junk food when they think no one is looking?

- ❀ Do you love going to friends or relatives houses because you can eat whatever you want without someone telling you you're not allowed to have it?

Do your answers give you the sense that you live in a family similar to Jodi's? The **Forbidden Foods** pattern makes it difficult to live in a world in which you are surrounded by all sorts of snack foods that are on the "no eating" list.

Aha! Now I Understand

It turns out that ever since Jodi was young, certain foods were "forbidden." Her parents had good intentions, trying to make sure Jodi and her brother ate only healthy foods. But kids who are never allowed to eat junk food often feel deprived. So they sneak food when their parents aren't watching. But your body doesn't know whether you're sneaking food or eating it openly. If you eat more food than your body needs to be healthy, the excess will turn into fat. And guess what, when foods are forbidden, people are likely to eat *more* of them when they do get the chance. Try this experiment:

1. Think of your favorite junk food (chocolate chip cookies, potato chips, pizza, a certain candy bar, etc.).

2. Now, tell yourself that you're not allowed to eat it EVER AGAIN!

3. Don't eat it for as long as you can. Hours? Days? Weeks? Months? How long can you hold out? How often do you think of the food? You probably can't stop thinking about it. Once you knew you couldn't have it, you wanted it desperately.

4. When you finally can't take it any more, can you eat just a little bit, or do you have the urge to stuff your face with as much as possible, because you know it's forbidden? (I'd be stuffing my face!!)

This experiment demonstrates that *when we are forbidden to eat certain foods we want these foods more than anything else.* If you grow up in a family that forbids certain foods, you are more likely to try and get these foods. And when you do get them, it might be difficult to eat just a little, so you'll eat as much as you can because you don't know when you'll have another chance to eat them again. And to make things worse, many girls add more and more things to their "forbidden" list as they get older, even if their parents are no longer watching so carefully.

Sometimes girls don't come from a Forbidden Foods family, yet they still develop the pattern themselves. This may happen when girls need to lose weight. For example, Celia (age 12) told me that she was sure that if people saw her eating cookies they would think she was a fat slob.

"Look at me," Celia exclaimed, "I'm enormous. No one thinks I should eat cookies or cake, even me. But I can't help myself. I try to stay away from junk food, but then when I can't take it anymore, I don't just eat one cookie, I'll have half the package."

Celia's relationship with Forbidden Foods isn't healthy because even though she is very overweight, depriving herself of the food she craves isn't stopping her from eating them. It's making her want them even more. It is important for anyone who eats like Celia, to make sure they don't have an eating disorder. If you think that your eating is very out of control or very secretive, make sure that you read Chapter 10, Understanding Eating Disorders (and Getting Help), and get help if you need it.

The First Step

Your parents may have a difficult time agreeing when you tell them that banishing junk food from your life is actually contributing to your weight struggles. So it might help you if you suggest that they read this section. Maybe they'll even learn something about their own eating patterns. Here's the plan—The Big C's (chips, cereal, candy, cookies, crackers, ice cream, and any other cravings):

- Ask to have some big C foods at home because not having any "fun" foods makes you feel deprived. You then think about these foods all the time, and eat lots of them whenever you get the chance.

- Explain that if you know the foods will always be there, you will be less likely to eat them all at once and you will do your best to eat only a little each day. If they seem reluctant, agree to try it for two months. NOTE: if your need for certain foods seems out of control, and this *doesn't* stop over a few weeks, read Chapter 10, Understanding Eating Disorders (and Getting Help), to figure out if you have an eating disorder.

🌸 Ask your parents not to show disapproval when you eat "junk food." Explain that you don't like to keep secrets or sneak eat, but that it is difficult for you to eat openly if they disapprove.

What If It Doesn't Work?

It is possible that neither reading nor a calm discussion will convince them to change things at home. They may still choose to have only "healthy" foods in the fridge and pantry and continue to voice disapproval of your wanting to eat "banned" foods.

While this will be frustrating, you need to accept that a parent is not required to agree with everything you do. His or her lifetime of patterns may make it difficult to change, or your parents may simply see things differently than you. BUT, this does not mean you should give up. Instead, accept the differences between you and your parents and then do it on your own. It won't be as easy without a parent's support, but if you work at it, you'll reach your goal.

Making the Changes

Your goal is to be able to eat The Big C's in moderation, without needing to stuff your face, to sneak eat, or to feel guilty. Achieving this goal will probably be a challenge because it requires you to undo a lifetime of negative associations with food and eating. I will give you a series of steps to follow. Be sure you master one before moving onto the next. And don't be surprised if it takes you weeks or even months to get through all the steps.

Step 1: Think about which food you deprive yourself of the most; the food you're likely to choose when you go off a "diet." Now, get yourself this treat. Once you have it, eat some or all of it, while telling yourself it is fine for you to eat foods you like, and good not to deprive yourself.

Step 2: When you have finished your Big C food (whether it takes an hour or a week) get more. Continue replacing it until your brain and body realize that you do not have to stuff your face because when foods you love are available, you won't feel deprived and you won't have to overeat.

Step 3: After you've tried this a few times, you can add other Big C foods that you love. Once you start to feel less guilty about eating your favorite foods, you won't feel the need to eat large amounts at a time.

Step 4: Even if your parents are concerned you're eating too much junk food, DON'T eat secretly. It's unhealthy for your body and soul. Instead, keep telling yourself: I'm not doing anything wrong; I'm helping myself to have a healthier relationship with food; I'm allowed to enjoy what I eat; I don't have to feel guilty; I don't have to feel ashamed. If you need to, write these statements on note cards and read them every day. Remember, you are in charge of making yourself healthier and happier, so take control of your choices and decisions.

When you are finally able to eat **Forbidden Foods** without feeling guilty, without eating secretly, and without needing to hide, you will have achieved an enormous goal. Getting there may be hard work, but it will be worth it. You might even find that your mom or dad wants to break the pattern and do it along with you.

Pattern #3: Snacking is Sweeter.

"**Suzie (age 16):** I've been in therapy with Dr. Susan for a while because she's been helping me deal with my parents' loud, screaming divorce. Lately, I've been discussing my weight with her. I know that my mother, sister, brother, and I were all very overweight. I also know that our home is the junk food capital of the world. What I can't figure out is, why?"

Suzie began to examine her family pattern of eating snack food. She decided that one of the best ways to find out why there was so much snack food in the house would be to ask her mom. As it turned out, Suzie's question prompted her mother to really think about the family's eating pattern. After she thought about it for a few days, she was very honest in her discussion with Suzie. In fact, not only did their talk help Suzie to understand her own less than healthy eating habits, but it also showed her mom that the whole family could benefit from breaking a bad pattern.

What about you? Do you come from a snacking family? Your answers to the following questions will give you a clue:

- Are the kitchen cabinets in your house stuffed with all kinds of snack foods?
- Are meals generally a second thought in your family, because no one is really hungry since they've been snacking throughout the day?
- Is the refrigerator mostly empty because cooking and preparing meals don't happen very often?
- Have you always lived in a home where a parent (or babysitter) doesn't really say "no" to snacking, no matter what time of day it is?

Aha, Now I Understand

After the divorce, Suzie and her siblings lived with their mom. Her mom explained that she felt terribly guilty about everything they'd been through. As a result of her guilt, Suzie's mom never wanted to say "no" to her children for any reason. When it came to food, they could eat what they wanted when they wanted. At meal times, Suzie was hardly ever hungry for healthy food because she'd been snacking so much in between, and anyway, her mom never really forced the kids to eat healthy meals, because she didn't want to upset them. And that's how they'd all gained a lot of weight. This is not a difficult pattern to uncover. All you need to do is recognize that in your family junk food has taken the place of real food too much of the time. If you realize that you have been growing up in a family that doesn't have enough boundaries about food and eating the following sections show you what to do.

The First Step

When you realize what has been going on in your family, ask your parents if they will start to buy fewer junk-food snacks and more healthy foods such as fruit, vegetables, string cheese, and nonsugary cereals. This may sound strange because often parents have to beg kids to eat less junk food and eat more fruit and vegetables. But in some families, parents may not have enough knowledge about how to eat healthily (maybe their parents didn't teach them). Or, as in Suzie's family, there may be emotional reasons that kids have tons of snack food, and not enough healthy food available. Whatever the reason, discuss it with your parents.

What If It Doesn't Work?

Your parents may find it difficult to buy food in a healthier way, or they may not want to deprive you or themselves of snack foods. So if you find that despite asking for healthier foods, more regular meal times, and some boundaries on snacking, these aren't happening, you're going to have to carefully read Chapter 12, Motivation Is A Must, to find an enormous amount of will power and do it on your own.

Making the Changes

Suzie was eventually able to pull herself out of junk-food haven, and find some healthy moderation in her eating. She didn't stop eating junk food all together, but she just ate less of it, included more healthy snacks, and ate regular meals, too. Here's the plan for success that I helped Suzie create. I'm sure you'll be able to do it, too:

Dr. Susan's Snacking Switch

1. Make a list of satisfying breakfast foods you enjoy, like cereal, a cheese sandwich, yogurt and fruit, and eggs—real food, not cake, cookies, granola bars, toaster pastries, and stuff like that. Then start to eat breakfast every day. *Your*

goal is to feel satisfied after eating breakfast so you won't want to snack soon after breakfast.

2. Begin eating lunch every day. For example, have a peanut butter and jelly sandwich, a slice of pizza or half a subway sandwich. *Your goal is to not let yourself get too hungry because then you will start craving junk food.*

3. Dinner may be a challenge if your mom or dad doesn't cook, or if healthy meals aren't a priority in your home. One alternative is to start cooking for yourself—really! It doesn't have to be anything fancy. You can make pasta, warm up soup, heat pizza bagels, or scramble eggs. You can even find easy cook books to try out. On the weekends you'll probably spend some time eating out with friends so look for healthy and substantial foods that will satisfy you and reduce your urge to snack later. For example, try pasta primavera, a slice of veggie pizza, stir-fried chicken or sautéed steak. For many more healthy eating suggestions, turn to Chapter 8, **The Real Road to a Healthier Body and Happier You**, and Chapter 9, **Healthy Eating Anywhere and Everywhere.** *Your goal is to make sure you don't let yourself slip back into snacking instead of eating real food.*

4. Make two lists of snack foods for when you are hungry between meals. The first is a list of healthy snacks (fruit, vegetables, string cheese, yogurt, dried fruit, nuts, peanut butter) and the other has all the "not so healthy" junk food that you've probably always eaten. For your first two snacks of the day, make sure to eat something from the healthy list. Then, for your third snack (if you need one) eat something from the other list. Make sure you have lots of things to choose from on your "healthy" list so you don't get bored. *The goal is to eat more healthy snacks.*

Pattern #4: Fast Living–Fast Food

"**Alexa (age 15):** I have to lose weight and I'm tired of thinking about it! I have two chins, my thighs rub together and I wouldn't be caught dead in a bathing suit without a T-shirt over it. But, in my family, it's impossible to lose weight because all we do is eat at fast food restaurants. It doesn't take a genius to know that this is no way to have a healthy body."

Alexa's family has a hectic lifestyle. Her mom and dad both work. At night, there's always homework and activities. They eat out or bring food in practically every day. The result is a pattern of Fast Living—Fast Food. Breakfast might be a donut or a muffin. Lunch is school food for Alexa and her sister (which in most schools means fried with a capital F, drowned in grease or pure rubber!). Dinner is Chinese, Italian, or fast food. Snacking is no different—a candy bar or an ice-cream cone. As long as it's quick and doesn't require clean-up, it works for them.

Figuring out if you come from a fast food family is really simple. Just answer the following questions and it'll become clear to you almost immediately:

* Do you (and your family) eat almost all meals on the run?
* Are your (and your family's) meals usually from a drive-thru?
* Do you eat whatever is fastest and most convenient, without much thought as to whether it's healthy?

Aha, Now I Understand

Unfortunately, eating like this all the time really does make it difficult to have a healthy body—for Alexa and for you. Alexa's doctor has been telling her and her parents for several years that she needs to lose weight.

Finally, Alexa got fed up with feeling bad about her body and decided to take a look at her family pattern. It was easy to see that eating lots of high fat, sugary fast food was not going to make her feel or look healthy. And as she got older, she also realized that it would be impossible to change her family's busy lifestyle. She knew she would have to change what she eats, taking charge of the menu herself.

The First Step

Alexa decided that on the nights they eat out or bring food in, she would make healthier choices. She began to do this by looking at menus carefully for items that are grilled, stir-fried, sautéed, baked, broiled, boiled or steamed. Breakfast and lunch could still be "fast" but she would figure out ways to make them more nutritious as well (she could start by bringing a sandwich and some fruit to school, rather than risking the cafeteria food). Her parents were very supportive and began going to the supermarket once in a while to purchase healthy school lunch foods. They also encouraged her to tell them which fast food restaurants she preferred for healthier choices. Alexa's only disappointment was that her parents didn't start to eat in a healthier way themselves, but she made a promise to herself to try not to do the same if she had kids.

What If It Doesn't Work?

If your parents are not supportive or if they think you are making things difficult for the family, you should still make the right choices for your life, no matter who—including your parents—stands in your way! So, if your doctor has told you that you need to lose weight, or simply because you know that the "fast-food lifestyle" is not healthy, then **take control of the menu and take control of your life!**

Making the Changes

You may not realize it, but it is possible to eat out, bring in, and eat fast food while still being healthy. Practically every restaurant and store has healthy items. You just need to **choose them!**

I won't list all the healthy choices here because Chapter 9 tells all about eating out healthily. But, I'd like to share two important tips that really helped Alexa:

1. Don't feel bad if you're eating out and you really can't find anything healthy because no one has to eat perfectly all the time. In fact, once in a while, if you want to eat the less healthy food then eat it! See Pattern #1 for the reason why.

2. When the choice of meals is up for decision, speak up about what *you* would like. What's more, don't be afraid to order foods your family doesn't usually like, and don't feel bad about ordering something healthy even if everyone else calls you a "health nut." Your healthy choices probably just remind them that theirs are unhealthy.

Pattern #5: Dieting and Denying

"Dominique (age 18): My mom always looks at her body and comments about how fat she is (not!). She's constantly either at the gym or eating salad. She has so much will-power and sometimes I feel like a fat slob next to her. But when I try to eat and exercise the way she does, I feel starving, tired and cranky."

"Melissa (age 14): Everyone tells me to eat less, especially my grandmother. She says the only way to have a beautiful body is to diet all the time. I want to have that kind of a body, but I don't think I can live without chocolate chip cookies."

Both Dominique and Melissa are experiencing one of the most difficult family patterns of all, where mom or both parents or even grandparents let you know you should be dieting in order to look and feel good. You may even feel this pressure from an older sister or from your friends. Sometimes, as in Dominique's family, the communicating is done by example. Her mom's extreme behavior makes Dominique believe this is the way everyone lives. Other times, as in Melissa's family, dieting is suggested as a helpful remedy for a girl's troubles.

Dieting and Denying is one of the most common family patterns to affect girls early in life and stay with them forever unless something is done to break the pattern. Think about it: At any given time more than 85 percent of teenage girls are dieting, or believe they should be. Wow! But it's not surprising because many girls grow up with mothers (and grandmothers) who diet all the time.

Well, I've got some news for you and them: DIETS DON'T WORK. Diets are very restrictive, so you feel deprived and miserable. Inevitably you break down and cheat which makes you feel more miserable. Then, you feel so bad that you give up the diet altogether and, guess what? Now you feel even worse. No wonder it's so hard to stick to a diet. In Chapter 7 we will discuss why diets don't work and what to do instead of dieting, but right now, it's important to figure out if your family, like Dominique or Melissa's, is in a Dieting and Denying pattern. To begin with, ask yourself the following questions:

* Is there always "diet" food in the house and does your mom or dad seem to live on salads, "fat-free" foods, and diet soda?

* Does your mom or dad weigh her or himself a lot and/or talk about wearing clothes that are "slimming"?

* Do your parents often talk about "dieting" or "losing weight" or has one of your parents suggested that you go on a diet?

* Does your parent make exercise a priority over almost anything else?

* Does your parent's weight yo-yo up and down?

* Does your mom or dad eat "junk food," but then feel too guilty or full to eat a real meal, or does she or he pick at food, rather than really eating it?

* Does your mom talk about not liking her body, or parts of her body? Does she frequently look at her self critically in the mirror or does she hide her body from you because she's ashamed of how she looks?

* Does your mom ask you, "Do I look fat in this?" Do you find yourself asking her the same question?

If you found that you answered "yes" to some or all of these questions, you are most likely in a Dieting and Denying family pattern. Because depriving yourself of food can make you lose weight, some parents seem to look healthy. But in reality, their body image and relationship with food is unhealthy. Other parents diet constantly but are still overweight. No matter what your parent looks like, the messages communicated by Dieting and Denying are not healthy.

It is likely that your mom, dad or others influencing you probably don't even realize they're communicating an unhealthy pattern. Rather, they are living the pattern that was communicated to them. For example, if your mom is super-concerned about whether she's thin, maybe her mom was either the same way, or her mom was very critical of her daughter's (your mom's) body when she was a teenager.

Aha! Now I Understand

Did you know that coming from a Dieting and Denying family pattern can actually make you gain weight? Really, it can! There are two ways that this can happen:

1. You go on many diets, but because it's so hard to deny yourself the foods you like (and you shouldn't have to), and you eventually eat more of them than you would have if you hadn't been dieting. This is similar to the Forbidden Foods pattern, so you might want to reread that section.

2. You rebel against the whole dieting thing and go crazy eating everything you want. Interestingly, this is especially common when you

don't get along well with your parents. For example, Remi (age 16) fought constantly with her mom. She knew that dieting, exercising, and being thin were very important to her mom, so just to spite her, she went in the other direction. She ate all the "non-diet" foods she could, and never exercised. It drove her mother crazy, which was Remi's goal. But as you can imagine, Remi's body became overweight and unhealthy.

The First Step

If you have one parent who is not in the **Dieting and Denying** pattern, I suggest that you show them this chapter and ask them for help. However, if both your parents (or if you only live with one parent) diet and deny then asking a parent for help may not be the first step. This is because when a parent is stuck in this pattern she or he probably won't be able to help you change your relationship with food. But you can try discussing it or showing them this chapter because perhaps you can help them to see that this isn't your problem alone. You may be surprised, maybe they will even agree with you.

What If It Doesn't Work?

It can be difficult to battle the message that you're supposed to diet, strive for thinness all the time, and exercise like crazy. But you need to know that *dieting is not healthy and neither is constantly being critical of your body. You don't need to make exercise a priority over everything else in your life, and your self-worth should not be decided by the scale or the mirror.* This is true even if adults (or anyone else) in your life lives this way. If these are the messages being communicated to you, break free now and move on.

Making the Changes

First, congratulations! You're taking a huge step by agreeing to break your dieting cycle. You're probably a bit nervous, wondering how you'll survive without a constant diet in your life, but I give you my promise that if you continue to follow all the ideas and tips in this book, everything will be awesome! So, here we go.

Dr. Susan's Five Steps to Your Diet-free Life

Step 1: Don't weigh yourself. If this seems impossible, limit it to once a week and expect normal monthly fluctuations of a few pounds. Better yet, get rid of your scale altogether.

Step 2: Look at yourself in the mirror once a day, every day and say something positive about a different part of your body. Some ideas are: "my eyelashes are really long," "I have pretty feet," "I rarely have a bad hair day," "I am happy with the shape of my breasts." This may not be an easy exercise at first, but keep working at it, each day.

Step 3: If you see your mom, dad, or other influential adult dieting, tell yourself: *This is not healthy behavior for me to copy.* In fact, as you become more aware of this, you will probably see it happening all around you—girls in school, articles in magazines, and stars on TV—all talking about dieting. This doesn't mean it's healthy for them either.

Step 4: If anyone suggests you go on a diet say this: *Thanks for worrying about me, but you may not realize that dieting is actually really unhealthy and hardly ever works. And, besides, I am making healthy changes so that I'll feel and look better.*

Step 5: Move on to Chapters 7, 8, and 9, which will teach you how to eat in a healthy way and lose weight without feeling deprived and, most importantly, without dieting.

Pattern #6: Sibling Stress

Samantha (age 17): I sometimes hate living in my family. My younger sister, Carin is a great athlete who eats whatever she wants and never gains a pound. Lucky Carin has the "good" genes from mom's side of the family. I, of course, inherited dad's genes— the ones that make me struggle with my weight. To make matters worse I hate sports. I know I should exercise, but I haven't found an exercise I like. I try to eat healthily and I am successful a lot of the time. But I still can't help being jealous of Carin, who seemed to have it so easy. Carin and I are always fighting with each other.**"**

For girls like Samantha who try to have a healthier body, it can be difficult to have a sister or brother looks exactly the way you would like to look seemingly without even trying. This often creates feelings of jealousy, envy, or anger toward your sibling, which can cause confusion and frustration in yourself and your family. I have an official name for these feelings—I call them **Sibling Stress**.

Sibling Stress can be a pattern that creeps into your relationship with your brother or sister without you even realizing it. It may be hard to admit to the jealousy or resentment so you may find yourself fighting, bickering, and griping at your sibling for all sorts of reasons that have nothing to do with what your bodies look like. Samantha's mother told me she thought Samantha hated her younger sister, but she had no idea why.

"Carin loves Samantha and really looks up to her," she explained. "But Samantha has no patience for her sister, argues with her about everything, and is mean to her. I just don't get it."

Sibling Stress is more common that most people like to admit. But if you answer yes to any (or all) of the following questions you should be able to admit, at least to yourself that you've got a problem with a sister or brother:

* ✳ Do you sometimes feel like you hate your sibling?

* ✳ Do you often wish you were just like your sibling?

* Will you sometimes find yourself becoming angry with your sibling for no real reason at all?

* Do you sometimes feel that your mom or dad favors your sibling because she or he is in some way, better than you?

* Are you relieved to be away from home, or wish that you were already, because it means you don't have to think about your jealous feelings?

* Do you think that your sibling has a better life than you because she or he has a better body than you?

Aha! Now I Understand

At first Samantha was reluctant to reveal her true feelings to her mother, saying instead that Carin was annoying, bratty, and whiny. But then she told me something different: "Carin is perfect. She looks great, eats whatever she wants and is athletic. But I constantly have to 'watch what I eat.' I don't like to exercise and I'm unhappy with my body. I'm angry at Carin all the time. I guess that's why I'm mean to her." Once Samantha realized what her behavior meant, life with Carin suddenly took a change for the better.

The First Step

Like Samantha, you will need to think about your relationship with your sibling and then take an honest look at your feelings, to determine whether you are in the middle of a pattern of **Sibling Stress**. If you do recognize these feelings you don't have to tell anyone else, but don't hide them from yourself.

Making the Changes

I won't lie to you, getting rid of **Sibling Stress** may not be the easiest thing you've ever done, especially if it's been going on for a long time. But you can definitely do it as long as you take the following steps and be patient with yourself.

Dr Susan's Sibling Stress Relief Plan

Step 1: Tell yourself the following: **Everyone is different and I will focus on what I love about myself, not what I dislike.** You may need to say this several times a day until you believe it.

Step 2: Make a list of all the positive things about yourself that you can think of. Then make the same kind of list for your sibling. Include things like: how you do in school (e.g., great in French and English), your friends (close friends, interesting friends?), your looks (pretty hair, eyes, etc.), talents (piano, tap, and all others), skills (like cooking, gardening, building), emotions (sensitive, easygoing, etc.). When you are done you will discover that your list of positive attributes is at least as long as the one you make for your brother or sister. Your sibling may have strengths in some areas (like eating and weight), but you have many strengths of your own. Every time you feel envious or angry look at your list and remind yourself that you're terrific.

Step 3: Make a list of the things about your sibling that make you jealous. Then, next to each item, write C (Control) if you can have control over changing the item about which you're jealous. C issues include: weight, hair color, mood, friendliness, knowledge, style of dress, academics, physical fitness. Write NC (No Control) next to the items that are impossible to change (except maybe with extreme measures, like plastic surgery). NC items are: height, breast size, body type, and foot size. As you do this you will notice that the list of C items is much longer than the list of NC items. You will also notice that many of the things that make you jealous are on the C list. This tells you that with effort and focus, you will be able to make changes in your own life so that you will have no need to feel jealous. Instead of feeling sorry for yourself when you think about your sibling, TAKE ACTION and start to change the C items. You'll soon find that the NC items don't even matter any more—trust me on this. It may not be easy, but it's *in your control to help yourself.* Just continue to read this book, and then take control!

What If It Doesn't Work?

If it's an enormous struggle to get rid of your jealousy or anger, try something different. Instead of working on the feelings first, do the steps backwards. Start making the changes in your eating and exercise habits first (the C areas). As you start to feel better about yourself, your **Sibling Stress** should fade quite quickly. If your feelings toward your sibling continue to interfere with your happiness, you should speak to an adult you trust (e.g., parent, school counselor, other relative) and ask for some help managing your feelings.

In the first part of this book we have covered many areas of emotional, social, genetic, and family issues that can interfere with you becoming healthier and looking better. Now that you're armed with knowledge and the ability to control your life, you're ready for the information and motivation that will help you make important healthy changes in eating and exercise.

Seven

On a Diet . . . Off a Diet—
The Rocky Road to a
Not So Healthy Body

Your Food Attitude

Does having a healthy body seem out of reach? If you struggle to make the right eating choices, you're probably confused with all the advice and diets in magazines, in books, and on TV. You've also probably tried many of these in an attempt to achieve the weight loss and happiness they promise. You may have also discovered that the promises for miraculous changes and lifelong happiness can be disappointing. If you're like many girls, your relationship with food and eating may be like a roller coaster:

* One week you swear by the success of a new and promising diet, but by the next, you've become disappointed that you don't have the willpower to stick with it.

* Another week begins with the promise to yourself that you'll eat only healthy food but on Saturday night you give in and eat three slices of pizza, a large soda, and a double scoop of peanut butter-chocolate chip ice cream.

❄ You tell your mom to throw out all the "unhealthy" food, but then you eat most of a box of fat-free cookies.

❄ You eat a low-fat granola bar for breakfast and a huge green salad for both lunch and dinner every day for two weeks and you wonder why you haven't lost any weight.

These are just a few examples of how girls try to lose weight. But, guess what? They don't work. Your attitude toward food and the eating choices you make, can have a huge impact on whether or not you succeed at achieving a healthier body. So, how is your food attitude and your knowledge about healthy eating? Take the following quiz to find out (remember not to write directly in a library book). Choose the answers that most closely resemble the real life choices and decisions you typically make.

1. You want to lose weight so you:

a. skip breakfast, eat ½ a cup of plain yogurt, and carrot sticks for lunch and a large salad for dinner

b. cut out or severely limit sugar and other carbohydrates (bread, pasta) and eat mostly protein (fish, cheese, meat, poultry) and vegetables.

c. continue to eat a variety of foods but reduce portion sizes, especially for sugary or high fat foods.

2. Everyone is talking about a great new diet. You:

a. try it immediately.

b. forget it—you're never been successful at trying to lose weight.

c. Find out if it's healthy for teenagers before deciding whether to try it.

3. Chocolate is your favorite food so you:

a. eat a whole chocolate bar at least once a day, maybe more often.

b. usually indulge your cravings with a mini-chocolate bar, chocolate cereal, or a chocolate lollipop.

c. never eat chocolate—it's bad for you, no matter how much you like it.

4. You never have time for a sit down meal. Instead you:

a. pack a sandwich and some fruit to eat on the run.

b. buy fast food or eat lots of snacks out of vending machines.

c. skip meals, but when you're starving you eat a lot to make up for it.

5. You hardly ever feel really hungry. This is probably because you

a. snack on candy, chips, pretzels, and ice-pops throughout the day.

b. eat several small, fairly healthy meals throughout the day.

c. have trained yourself to ignore hunger pangs.

6. When there's good food around you'll

a. eat if you're hungry. Or, if you're not hungry you'll have a taste of something delicious.

b. keep eating until there's nothing left, even if you're not hungry.

c. resist the food but think about eating it the whole time.

7. When you come home from school you want something to eat because

a. you're starving since you haven't eaten anything since breakfast.

b. you want a small snack before beginning your homework.

c. home and eating always go hand in hand.

8. Fat-free food

a. is always healthier than regular food—so it's better for you.

b. is lower in calories than regular food—so you can eat as much as you want.

c. has about the same calories as regular food—the words "fat free" make you think it's lower calorie.

9. Being a vegetarian is

    a. always healthier than being a meat-eater.

    b. less healthy than being a meat-eater.

    c. can be healthy if you do it right.

10. Fast food

    a. can be healthy if you make the right selections.

    b. is never healthy.

    c. is always healthy.

Healthy responses: Give yourself a point for every correct response, then add up your points.

1. c	2. c	3. b	4. a	5. b
6. a	7. b	8. c	9. c	10. a

	Answer	Score		Answer	Score
1.			7.		
2.			8.		
3.			9.		
4.			10		
5.			11.		
6.			12.		**TOTAL**
			+		=

Scoring

Nutritionally Knowledgeable (7–10 points): Congratulations! You realize that eating all foods in moderation is the way to go and that depriving yourself (dieting and starving your body) won't make you healthy. So what is standing in your way of living a healthy lifestyle and feeling good about your body? Perhaps you have the knowledge but still don't make the healthiest choices. As you read this chapter, you will figure out how to power your knowledge into a healthy body!

Address your attitude (4-6): You have some knowledge about healthy eating, but not quite enough. You still need a few tools to help you build a healthier lifestyle. This chapter will teach you how to make steady changes in your attitude towards food and eating. Soon, you'll feel smarter as well as healthier.

Change your choices (0-3 points): You are heading down a slippery slope. Your eating patterns cycle between self-deprivation and overindulgence. You need to be better armed with knowledge about how food can help you become healthy. You also need to learn how to change your attitude toward eating so that you don't continue to harm your body and hurt yourself emotionally. This chapter will give you all the support you need to jump off the slippery slope and start taking controlled steps on the more level road towards a healthier and happier you.

Now, look no further, because this chapter will teach you all you need to know about healthy and unhealthy eating. We'll start off with one of the great mysteries of food and eating—CALORIES!

The 411 on Calories

You hear about calories everywhere. Foods and drinks brag about being "low calorie" or "no calorie." Your mother talks about "cutting" them, your friend says you can "burn them off" and your health teacher says you should "watch them." So, what exactly are calories? From everything you've seen, it might seem that calories are a bad thing and the fewer you get the better, right? Actually, no—calories are an important part of life and we need them to survive. But it is true that too many calories can be unhealthy? Confused? Okay, here is a crash course in calories and what they do for you.

The word calorie actually has two meanings. First, a calorie is a measure of food and drink you *take in*; and second, a calorie is a measure of energy *used up* by your body.

Let's look at the first meaning. When you eat or drink something, the number of calories is the *amount of energy that the food or drink gives your body to use.* These are the calories that your body *takes in*. The number of calories you take in each day is determined by what you eat and how much. The number of calories in a certain food does NOT indicate whether or not it is healthy. Rather, the health of a food is determined by how much nutrition it gives your body. But, all foods, even less healthy ones, have a place in the life of a healthy eater. The key is in balancing all the types of food you eat. As we'll discuss later, your body needs many different nutrients to grow healthily. This is why you should eat a variety of foods. When it comes to calories you need to eat enough of them to fuel your growth and functioning.

Secondly, calories are a measure of energy that your body *uses*. This is sometimes called "burning" calories. You've probably heard people say that you "burn calories even when you sleep" and wondered if it's true. It is true, because even while sleeping, your body uses up calories for basic functions such as breathing, digestion, pumping blood, growing, and healing. You also burn calories by any type of movement. Walking, talking, laughing, learning, flirting, eating, dancing, typing, reading, and all other activities use up calories. The more you move the greater the number of calories your body uses. For example, exercise uses up many more calories than watching TV.

It is important to eat enough calories to fuel the functioning and growth of your body *as well as* to give you energy for living life to the fullest. In other words, your body needs a certain amount of energy (number of calories) every day to maintain its functioning and to keep you going. But since all people are different, the amount of food your body needs is unique. There are a few things that determine how many calories your body needs each day to maintain itself.

1. **Activity level** (whether you're a couch potato, very active or somewhere in between). The more active you are, the more calories your body requires, because activity uses up calories. In Chapter 11 we will discuss this in greater detail.

2. **Metabolism.** This is the process by which your body uses up calories (energy) to fuel the functions that keep you alive (breathing, digesting, pumping blood, etc.). As you know from earlier chapters, everyone's body is different. If you have a fast metabolism your body uses up calories quickly and efficiently, and you are less likely to gain weight. Ectomorphs (remember them from Chapter 3?) usually have fast metabolisms. If you have a slow metabolism, you are likely to gain weight more easily because your body doesn't use up the calories as efficiently (mesomorphs may have slower metabolisms).

3. **How much muscle you have.** The muscular parts of your body use up more calories than the fatty parts of your body. This is because muscle actually uses energy just to maintain itself. So, if you tend to have a somewhat more muscular body (or if you decide to develop one by exercising!), you will need to eat more calories to maintain your healthy body.

Now, I'm sure you must be wondering what it means if your body has more (maybe much more) fat than it should have. This is an important question, so to answer it, I consulted with an expert when it comes to girls and calories—Dr. Judy Marshel. Dr Marshel is an awesome nutritionist who works with tons of teenage girls. She'll be giving us advice throughout this chapter (you can read more about Dr. Marshel at the end of the book). She says that if your body has more fat than you would like, it probably means that the amount of energy you take in (as calories) is greater than the amount of energy you use up (as calories). This is because calories that are not used as energy get stored by your body as fat.

It's simple subtraction. If you eat 2000 calories a day and use up (burn) only 1500, the extra 500 will be stored as fat. One pound of body weight equals 3500 calories, so if you eat 500 extra calories each day for one week you will gain a pound (500 calories x 7 days = 3500 calories or one pound). As you can imagine, if you eat like this for several months or several years, you can find yourself with a great deal more fat on your body than you'd like.

Dr. Marshel explained that the key to having a healthy body is to find a balance between eating and drinking enough calories to have energy for life and growth, and not eating so many that you end up with more fat on your body than you need to be healthy.

As you know, many girls (and women) find it difficult to figure out how to do the second part—not eat too much. To help them eat less, they often turn to dieting as a way to reduce the number of calories they eat. These girls hope to lose weight or to stop gaining weight by eating fewer calories than they use up. So, Dr. Marshel, does dieting work?

Diets Don't Work!

"Yvonne (age 16): My doctor told me to lose at least twenty pounds, so I went on a diet. I cut out all junk food, ate only very low fat foods and completely stopped eating pizza and pasta (my favorites!). After about three weeks, I'd lost some weight, but the problem was that I couldn't take it any more, so I stopped. Two weeks later I'd gained it all back. It was so frustrating.**"**

Like Yvonne, many girls feel that dieting is their only hope for losing weight and becoming healthier. This is because going on a diet seems to be the key to looking and feeling great. BUT this is simply not true! As you may know from experience, dieting rarely does what it's supposed to do. It might help you lose weight fairly quickly (by causing you to take in fewer calories than you use up), but if you're like most people *you just gain the weight back when you go off the diet*. As soon as you stop dieting, you start eating more calories than you burn off, and before long the pounds are back on again. This is because diets don't teach you how to permanently change your poor eating habits into good ones. They only give you a temporary solution that ends when you end the diet.

Furthermore, when you diet, you lose weight quickly because you deprive yourself of many foods, thereby cutting out many calories. But, it's very difficult to permanently deprive yourself of foods you like—*and you shouldn't have to*. In fact, one of the main reasons diets don't work is that *you can't take the deprivation, so you go off the diet and gain back everything you lost (and sometimes more!)*.

"Jodi (age 15): My New Year's resolution was to lose thirty pounds by the summer, so I began a very strict diet that made me count the calories of everything I ate, and not go over a thousand calories a day. I hated it because I was always hungry, tired, and depressed, but I felt I had no choice. Except that I became more miserable as the days went by. My hair started falling out, my nails were cracking, I had headaches and I never had energy. Also, every time I "cheated" I felt guilty and a failure. It was really bad.

I'd been on the diet about six weeks when I went to my doctor for a check-up. She complimented my weight loss, but when I explained how I'd done it, she told me to stop immediately. She explained that restricting calories so much might make you lose weight, but that it is very bad for you and can cause many problems.

First, she said a girl needs a certain amount of calories to grow and live actively. I wasn't getting nearly enough, which is why I was feeling tired, hungry, depressed, and all the other stuff. She also said that a girl's body needs a variety of foods to be healthy. Most diets make it difficult to get that variety because they are too restrictive. Next, diets are created for adults, not teens or preteens, so they don't take into consideration that teens need more food than adult to be healthy. When a girl uses a diet that was created for adults, she deprives her body of nutrients it needs to grow healthily. This is true whether you are thin, fat or somewhere in between. She sent me to Dr. Susan who taught me how eat enough food to be healthy, but still lose weight slowly and safely by exercising and eating the right foods. I hope my experience helps other girls realize they have to learn to eat healthily and not learn how to diet. Dieting is bad for your body and especially for the way you feel about yourself.**"**

How Dieting Can Even Make You Gain Weight!

You go on a diet and lose fifteen pounds. You're psyched, proud of yourself, and feeling fine. And then you go off the diet—a normal response once you're feeling good. But, uh-oh, what happens? It is three months later and you've gained back everything you lost AND another five pounds. So . . . you're back on the diet again. This time you manage to lose ten pounds and you're cool again. You stop dieting and . . . you got it! The weight is back on again plus a little extra. It's easy to see that this pattern is not going to make you thinner, healthier or happier, but why does it happen?

When you diet, you send your body a message that it must begin to drastically reduce the amount of food or calories (energy) it has available to fuel your daily living. Your body interprets the message as "I'm about to be starving so I'm going to slow down, conserve energy, and hold onto as much of this food as possible by converting it to fat, because who knows when I'll get my next good meal."

During the cavewoman days, this worked nicely, because cave people often went without food for long periods of time if the hunting didn't go well. But it doesn't work for us, because when you stop dieting and go back to your old ways of eating (and not exercising), your body doesn't necessarily speed up its metabolism when it gets more food. For a while at least, it continues to store food as fat so you gain back the weight (and the extra pounds). To avoid this, it's important not to give your body the message that you're going to starve it. Then it won't go into the "fat storage" mode. The only way to do this is to eat healthily, without cutting too many calories.

If the Diet Doesn't Tell Me to Cut Calories, Is It Okay?

"Amelia (age 17): I went on one of those high protein, low carb diets and at first I was dropping weight like crazy. But after two weeks it was torture because I couldn't eat anything when I was out with my friends. Also I began to feel weak and light-headed a lot, so I stopped the diet. Of course, I gained back all the weight! It was so frustrating."

Many diets don't specifically tell you to eat fewer calories. Instead they tell you to eat or not eat certain foods or to eat in a special way. A diet like this may not even call itself a diet, so it may be difficult at first to realize that it is one. This doesn't mean it's any healthier for you than eating a drastically reduced number of calories. In fact, sometimes it can be even worse. A good rule to follow is that if a weight loss technique sounds too good to be true, it probably is. The creators of these weight loss plans try to sell their program by promising that they are better, easier, and faster than all other programs and that they will make you a happier, better person. This is no different than clothes manufacturers that try to make you believe that you will be happier in their clothes. You know that this is simply not true. Real happiness certainly doesn't come from a diet or a new outfit! But, if you find yourself tempted by seductive advertising, here are a few tips. AVOID any weight loss programs or diets that:

* Promise immediate, dramatic, and probably unrealistic results

* Show drastically different "before" and "after" pictures

* Promise weight loss of more than two pounds a week

* Promise significant weight loss without exercising at all

* Include quotes from people who have had fabulous results (in fact, it is illegal to do this!)

* Use words and phrases like "miraculous," "phenomenal," "dramatic," "breakthrough," "ancient," "supplements," "delicious shakes," "just discovered," "requires no effort" or "melts fat while you sleep"

* Promise the road to "true and lasting happiness" or something similar

Jaime, one of the girls in my **Girls Advisory Group**, felt it wasn't enough to include only these tips about diets to avoid. She suggested that I include specific types of diets that are commonly found in books, on TV, and in magazines. So here goes:

High-Protein, Low-Carbohydrate Diets

These diets are based on the theory that people gain weight by eating too many carbohydrates (like pasta, bread, rice) so the diet tells you to drastically restrict the amount of carbs you eat, but let you eat as much protein (meat, poultry, fish, cheese) as you like. These diets are unhealthy for you because your growing body requires a wide variety of all kinds of nutrients. Besides, the bottom line is that too many calories make you gain weight. It doesn't matter whether you get these calories from protein, carbohydrates or anywhere else. The key is to find foods that you like and that satisfy you, without eating too few or too many calories.

Liquid Diets

These are usually very low-calorie diets that tell you to drink "shakes" to replace the food you're not eating. Although it may be tempting to think you're getting "all the nutrients you need from a delicious shake" while still losing weight, this is simply not true. Further more, you probably realize that a liquid diet doesn't help you learn healthy eating habits that you can use for the rest of your life.

Specific Food Diets

Diets that tell you to eat a lot of one kind of food, like grapefruit, cabbage or rice are not at all well-balanced, not healthy, and very boooooring. Stay away!

No Fat Diets

There's a lot of talk these days about "cutting fat" and just about every aisle in the supermarket boasts products that are "fat free." But did you know that your body needs fat to function and grow? Furthermore, one of the best ways to lose weight healthily and keep the weight off is to eat some fat. This is because a fat-free diet is not only boring, it also makes you feel hungry all the time, both of which will cause you to go back to your unhealthy, very high fat eating and then gain back the weight. The key is to choose which fats you eat. We will discuss this in the next chapter.

Eat at Certain Times Diets

Diets that tell you to restrict eating to a certain time of day, tell you not to eat between meals, allow you to eat "junk food" for one hour a day, or require any kind of time constraints on your eating, are, like all other diets, trying to limit your calorie intake. This type of eating is not healthy for you because you need to pay attention to your hunger—eat when your body tells you it needs food. You can learn how to do this in Chapter 6.

Extremely High Fiber Diets

Foods that are high in fiber are filling and healthy, and should be a part of your eating plan. They help keep your body functioning well and satisfy your hunger. BUT, a diet that focuses only or mostly on high-fiber foods is no better than any other diet. Too much fiber can give you stomach cramps and diarrhea. Besides, eating a lot of fiber does not mean you will lose weight.

Really Dangerous Diets

Some girls become really desperate to lose weight, so they take extremely drastic measures, which may or may not cause weight loss, but which are *very* dangerous for their health. If you have ever been tempted by any of the following weight-loss techniques, STOP and reconsider. No matter how much you want to lose weight, each of these methods can cause serious illness, critically damage your body and even kill you. If you are currently involved in using any of these, stop reading right now and get help. You should start by going to Chapter 10 for suggestions to help yourself.

Laxatives

These are tablets, powders or drinks that, if used incorrectly or taken in excess, cause diarrhea and the frequent need to go to the bathroom. They can cause a little weight loss because some of the food you eat doesn't get absorbed. They also cause you to lose a great deal of fluid, as diarrhea. This can make you feel like you've lost weight, but you really haven't. Long term use of laxatives can be physically addictive. Your body becomes so used to them that if you try to stop using them, you become constipated. Since laxatives interfere with your body's ability to absorb food, you don't get many of the necessary nutrients that you need to grow healthily. You may also become psychologically addicted to laxatives—you feel that you can't function without using them. As you can imagine, long-term abuse can be serious and dangerous and can impact on you for many years.

Ephedra (Ma Huang)

This herb (usually found in pills, powders or liquids) speeds up your metabolism, which can cause weight loss, but with *extremely dangerous* side effects. Ephedra use causes your heart to pump too hard and fast and your blood pressure to go too high. You can become nervous, irritable, and have trouble sleeping. Ephedra has been linked to DEATH in many people, due to heart failure. Luckily, in some states Ephedra has become illegal and is no longer available. However, there are similar formulations still available, which are equally harmful and should be avoided at all costs. You must READ INGREDIENTS ON WEIGHT LOSS PRODUCTS to determine what you could be putting into your body. If you aren't sure of a product or an ingredient, ask your doctor before using it.

Diet or Weight Loss Pills

These pills usually contain large amounts of caffeine, which can speed up your metabolism temporarily. But, caffeine has lots of other nasty side effects, such as trouble falling asleep (even if you take it early in the day), jitters, nervousness, hyperactivity, and the big crash, which comes when the caffeine wears off—making you sleepy, cranky, and giving you a whopping headache. The amount of caffeine found in diet pills is way too much for any teenager to be consuming. Aside from caffeine, diet pills also frequently contain Ephedra (see above.)

Coffee

It, too, has caffeine and is bad for you in large amounts. If you love the taste of coffee, limit yourself to one or two cups early in the day and then stick to decaf the rest of the day. By the way, tea, some sodas, and chocolate milk also have caffeine as do many over-the-counter products such as Excedrin and some cold remedies. Don't forget these when you're considering how much caffeine you've had in a day.

Cigarettes

Did you know that number of cigarette smokers is increasing in teenage girls faster than in any other group? There are many reasons for this, one of which is that it gives you something to do with your mouth instead of eating. Some girls would rather be thin than live long healthy lives. The fact is that if you're smoking to "look good" or "keep the weight off," you're trading a few pounds now, for a few (or many) years of your life later—and the later may not be so far away. Lung cancer can happen at any time, not just to really old people. You're also trading a few pounds for bad breath, difficulty breathing, a hacking cough, and a decreased ability to fight germs—this is right now, not in the future. Ask yourself if it's worth it. If your answer is "yes" you should consider getting help, not only to stop smoking, but also to deal with the possibility that you have an eating disorder (read Chapter 10).

Cocaine, "Speed," and other Illegal Drugs

Certain illegal drugs work like caffeine and Ephedra to speed up your metabolism, which is also what causes the temporary "high" that you experience. I'm sure I don't need to tell you how bad these drugs are for you and that once you become addicted to them (which can happen very easily, without you even realizing it), they will ruin your life. If you're considering them, please, please stay away and if you're already using them, please get some help (see Appendix 2).

Steroids

More and more girls, it seems, have tried using bodybuilding (male) steroids—not to develop muscles, but to try and lose weight and reduce the amount of fat on their bodies—basically to get thin. Steroids can come as pills, shots, and creams (they're the same ones that have created scandals in major league baseball and other sports) and they are very, very dangerous! Girls who use these kind of steroids are at higher risk for heart attacks, strokes, and cancer. In addition, the side effects of steroids can include: developing a deep voice, depression, really serious problems with anger control, hair on your face and body, and serious acne.

Alcohol

Some girls feel that if they drink alcohol at social gatherings, instead of eating, they will lose weight since they will be avoiding the calories of food. Not true. Alcohol contains calories. In fact, beer, wine coolers, and exotic drinks can be high in calories—you've heard of a "beer belly" right? Also, if you get drunk or even just "buzzed," your inhibitions will be lowered (even if you don't realize it). Aside from really bad decision making (like drunk driving or drunk sex), this "buzz" can actually cause you to eat more because your impulses and good judgment are much lower. Other girls believe that alcohol helps them lose weight because it is a diuretic (makes you urinate a lot). Although alcohol is a diuretic, its effects are temporary, not affecting your real weight. The bottom line: for lots of reasons, it's better not to drink alcohol at all. But if this isn't a choice you're willing to make, limit your consumption and drink very slowly. And whatever you do, DON'T DRINK AND DRIVE, DON'T GET INTO THE CAR WITH SOMEONE WHO HAS BEEN DRINKING, AND DON'T HAVE SEX WHEN YOU'VE BEEN DRINKING. Of course, this applies to other mind-altering substances as well. I know this last advice seems off the topic, but in order to be happy and have a healthy body, you need to be alive and free of terrible illnesses, so it really is relevant.

Still Not Convinced?

So, you're still not sure that going on a diet is actually a sure-fire way to *gain* weight, or develop an eating disorder. Well then you may be interested to know that an important medical study found that normal-weight girls who dieted were five times more likely to end up overweight than girls who didn't diet. What's more, another study found that when overweight women diet a lot, they feel unhappy with their whole lives. Frequent dieting can also cause depression, and a lifetime of yo-yo dieting can even decrease your lifespan. If this isn't enough to get you to stay away from dieting, it's probably because you haven't figured out a successful and healthy alternative. Well, I've got one for you, so keep reading.

The Real Road to a Healthier Body and Happier You

Replace Dieting with Real Eating

"**Martina (age 14):** I stay away from crazy diets because I know they're unhealthy. But my doctor said I have to lose weight. So now I eat half a bagel and cream cheese for breakfast, some carrots, celery, and cucumbers for lunch, a couple of rice cakes and a can of diet soda after school so I don't get hungry. Then I eat the dinner my mom makes, but I try not to eat too much. It's been a couple of weeks and I've lost some weight. I guess it's working, right?"

Martina knows she should stay away from diets. But she doesn't realize that her attempt to have a healthier body is actually going to backfire because of her new eating choices. Like many girls, Martina thinks that to lose weight and become healthier, you need to drastically cut the amount of food (calories) you eat and replace it with carrots, celery, air-popped popcorn, rice cakes, apples, and diet soda. This is absolutely NOT TRUE. If you eat too few calories your body will go into starvation mode and store calories as fat (remember this from Chapter 7) so there's a good chance that you will not even lose as much weight as you would like to lose. Even if you do lose weight, eating this way for more than a day or two will drastically deprive your body and brain of the nutrients needed to be healthy and to think clearly. When you deprive your body of the calories and nutrients it needs, you will find yourself with little energy for activities and you will also find it difficult to concentrate on schoolwork or other interests you have.

Instead, I will offer you a healthier and *effective* way to lose weight. There are four simple things to do in order to lose weight and fat and become healthier. Each of these is an important step toward successfully transforming your poor eating patterns into healthier ones for the rest of your life. They work together to give you the control you need to feel happier about your body. I call them:

Four Fabulous Food Factors

1. Make healthier food choices

2. Eat smaller portions

3. Eat enough food

4. Eat foods you like, and don't deprive yourself of foods you love

I will discuss each of the Four Factors in detail so you learn how to use them in your life. As you break away from old eating habits and patterns, and become aware how your feelings, self-esteem, family, friends, and body image can affect your eating, it will be important for you to include all of the Four Fabulous Food Factors in your new lifestyle. You can work on them all at once or one at a time. Once you can consistently apply all four to your life, you *will* have control and feel better.

But remember you didn't gain the weight overnight, so be patient with yourself and keep working at it because now you have *Dr. Susan's Girls-Only Weight Loss Guide* to get it done!

Fabulous Factor One: Make Healthier Food Choices

Many girls are overweight because they don't choose healthy foods often enough. But you may not know how to determine if a food is healthy. There are four categories to consider when deciding how healthy a food is for you to eat. I call these categories the Main Menu, Consume with Care, Largely Liquid and Sweets and Treats. Each category should be included in your life in a different way.

The Main Menu

The foods in this category give your body energy (calories) it needs to function and grow. These foods fall into many groups, providing your body with the variety of nutrients (protein, carbohydrates, fat, fiber, vitamins, and minerals) it requires, without overdoing the fat or calories. I asked Dr. Marshel (our awesome nutritionist) to give us all the information we need about the Main Menu foods, so here goes.

Protein

Poultry, meat, fish, dairy, beans, eggs, soy, lentils, and *nuts* provide your body with protein, which:

→ Has *vitamins* and *minerals* necessary for healthy growth

→ Builds, repairs, and maintains muscles and all other tissues

→ Helps grow and maintain your bones, teeth, hair, and fingernails

→ Transports nutrients in and out of cells

→ Helps maintain a healthy immune system
(so you don't get sick easily)

→ Is a major part of all your hormones and digestive enzymes

It is important to note that many healthy proteins can be disguised in a way that makes them less healthy. For example, healthy chicken or fish becomes less healthy when you deep-fry them in cooking oil, adding lots of extra fat. Later in this chapter and in Chapter 9, we'll discuss this in detail.

Carbohydrates and Fiber

Some carbohydrates are healthy while others are less healthy. For example, sugar (and any food very high in sugar) is a type of carbohydrate that contains very few nutrients, so it is less healthy. It tastes good, but because it isn't nutritious, it doesn't fill us up, so we keep eating more and more. We'll talk more about sugar in the **Sweets and Treats** section. Foods like *pasta, rice, potatoes,* and *bread* are nutritious carbohydrates, which provide your body with fuel to energize you throughout the day. Look for whole grain (it should say so on the label) foods because they have more *vitamins, minerals,* and *fiber* than other similar foods. *Fruits* and *vegetables* are also carbohydrates that give you energy, and fiber, to help your body digest food. In addition, fruits and vegetables provide your body with *vitamins* and *minerals.* If fresh vegetables aren't available, frozen veggies are good, too. Canned veggies aren't bad, although they are higher in salt/sodium (too much isn't great for you) and have less fiber than fresh or frozen vegetable. Fruit juice has no fiber.

Some fruits and vegetables are camouflaged so you may not realize you're eating something healthy. For example, pizza sauce gives you the benefit of tomatoes, onions, and garlic. On the other hand, like proteins, it's also possible to disguise healthy fruits and vegetables so that they become less healthy. For example, tempura is Japanese style deep fried vegetables. The deep frying adds tons of extra fat.

Healthy Fats

Believe it or not, everybody needs to eat fat! Many people think it is okay or even good to eat little or no fat. But this is simply NOT TRUE!! You need fat in your diet to be healthy. Additionally, foods that contain fat are more satisfying to your taste buds and your stomach than fat-free foods. For example, you may find yourself eating a whole box of fat-free cookies because they just don't satisfy you the way regular cookies do, both emotionally and physically. You keep taking another hoping to find that satisfying cookie taste. But it doesn't happen because your body is searching for the fat. And guess what? *The fat-free cookies don't really have significantly fewer calories than the regular ones, because the fat is replaced with sugar.* Otherwise they'd be really disgusting! So you may end up eating more fat-free cookies than you would if you stuck to the regular, which would probably satisfy your taste buds after just one or two. You might find it helpful to reread Chapter 6, Pattern #2, to remind yourself of how denying yourself what you really want can actually prevent you from eating healthily or losing weight.

But, fat in your diet is tricky because some types of fat aren't as healthy as other types. For example, the kind of fat found in cookies, cake, red meat, butter, mayonnaise, whole milk or other full-fat dairy products is not as beneficial as the types of fats found in *fatty fish* (e.g., salmon, mackerel, bluefish, sardines), *nuts, seeds,* and *some vegetables,* like *avocados* and *olives.* These fats are important because they:

※ Keep your skin and hair healthy

※ Help you heal wounds

※ Maintain a healthy nervous system

※ Make hormones

※ Slow down digestion and the emptying of food out of your stomach, so you feel satisfied for longer. So, if you only eat no-fat or very low-fat foods, you will feel hungry all the time so you will eat more often. This could actually result in you eating more calories than if you included some fat in your eating plan.

The key is to eat mostly healthy fats, and balance them with enough protein and healthy carbohydrates. Keep reading and you'll see what I mean.

Consume with Care

The foods in this group have some healthy nutrients. But they may also have lots of calories, lots of fat, or both. Regular pizza is a good example of a Consume with Care food. The sauce is made of healthy vegetables and the cheese has some protein and calcium. But mozzarella cheese also has the less healthy kind of fat. These foods should definitely be a part of your new eating plan, but they should be balanced with foods that have healthy fats. Some other examples of Consume with Care foods are:

* Chicken with skin and fatty red meat (which have protein, but lots of fat)
* Full-fat (not low-fat or nonfat) dairy products (hard cheese, cottage cheese, yogurt, cream, sour cream) and peanut butter, all of which have protein but, *when eaten in excess*, a lot of fat
* Creamy pasta sauces (if you use *a lot* of sauce you're getting tons of fat)

Largely Liquid

The third category, Largely Liquid, consists of foods such as celery, lettuce, spinach, green peppers, cucumbers, and radishes, which are made mostly of water. Most have good nutritional value, and all have very few calories. These should definitely be included in your new eating plan but, no matter how tempting it is to do so, they should *never* take the place of foods in the Main Menu or Consume with Care categories.

Foods like this may be low in calories but they should be an addition, not a substitution.

Sweets and Treats

The last category, Sweets and Treats includes foods that taste good, but provide little or no nutritional value for your body. And, unlike the Largely Liquid foods, these are not low or no calorie. You may hear these types of foods referred to as "empty calories" because they don't give your body nutrients, but they do have lots of extra calories from sugar or fat. These are the foods that we all love, and usually eat too much and too often. Along with Consume with Care foods, too many *sweets and treats* can cause you to become overweight or overfat. Examples of foods in this category are cookies, potato chips, ice-cream, cake, candy, and pie.

Despite the fact that they are not nutritious, you *should not* stop eating these foods completely because you may feel deprived, frustrated, and resentful. There is a place in your life for every type of food, including "junk-food." When you read the other four Fabulous Factors, you will learn how to incorporate these foods into your new eating plan.

The Quiz

Let's see how much you've learned. Below is a list of twenty foods. Next to each one (on separate paper if it's a library book), determine which of the four categories it fits into, by writing:

MM for Main Menu, CC for Consume with Care, LL for Largely Liquid or ST for Sweets and Treats.

1. _____ Cheerios and low-fat milk
2. _____ French toast
3. _____ Spaghetti and ground turkey meatballs
4. _____ Corn on the cob
5. _____ Red licorice
6. _____ Peanut butter and jelly sandwich

7. _____ Tuna salad (with mayonnaise) in pita bread

8. _____ Large salad made with lettuce, sprouts, and cucumbers

9. _____ Chocolate covered strawberries

10. _____ Broiled fish (any kind) and a plain baked potato

11. _____ Chinese fried rice

12. _____ Chocolate milk

13. _____ Barbecued chicken and rice

14. _____ Diet Soda

15. _____ Bagel and cream cheese

16. _____ Cheeseburger and fries

17. _____ Movie popcorn with butter

18. _____ Chicken nuggets

19. _____ Orange juice

20. _____ Fruit salad

Scoring key

1. MM	2. CC	3. MM	4. MM	5. ST
6. MM	7. CC	8. LL	9. CC	10. MM
11. CC	12. CC	13. MM	14. LL	15. CC
16. CC	17. ST	18. CC	19. CC	20. MM

Scoring: Give yourself one point for each correct answer and add up your points.

16–20 points: You've really got the knowledge! Now you just need to apply it *consistently* to your life

11–15 points: You're almost there. Before you choose foods, make sure you've brushed up on the new information.

6–10 points: You'll be just fine as soon as you go through this section carefully, making sure you understand how foods differ from each other.

0–5 points: After you've read this information a few more times, take the quiz again and see your score shoot up.

Sensational Substitutions (Part I)

Just because a food isn't in the Main Menu category, doesn't mean you can't make it healthier. There are some wild ways that foods can be moved around, substituted and changed to make them more nutritious. Take the quiz list, for example. Although, we can't improve all of the foods, here are some easy ways to make many of them healthier:

French toast: For the batter, use skim or low-fat milk instead of whole milk, egg substitute instead of whole eggs, and 100-percent whole wheat instead of white bread. Use only a tiny splash of syrup for taste.

Peanut butter and jelly sandwich: Use all natural peanut butter (read the label to make sure peanuts are the *only* ingredient), 100-percent whole wheat bread, and real fruit jam instead of jelly.

Tuna salad in pita bread: Instead of regular mayonnaise mix tuna with a bit of mustard, low-fat mayonnaise or Italian salad dressing, and add some lettuce, tomatoes, and sprouts. Don't forget the whole wheat pita!

Large salad with lettuce, sprouts, and cucumber: Add a can of tuna or salmon or some grilled chicken or turkey. Nix the creamy dressings and go for a little olive oil and vinegar or low-fat dressing instead.

Chocolate covered strawberries: Try plain strawberries with a touch of powdered sugar.

Chinese fried rice: Go for the plain brown rice, mixed with vegetables (in a restaurant ask for "no oil").

Chocolate milk: Use skim or low-fat milk and less chocolate.

Diet soda: Although diet soda technically falls into the Largely Liquid category, Dr. Marshel pointed out that it really shouldn't be compared to vegetables, which are actually good for you! Diet soda may not have calories or fat, but it is full of chemicals, caffeine, and artificial sweeteners. Instead, go for water flavored with a splash of lemon or cranberry juice or flavored seltzer.

Bagel and cream cheese: Make sure your bagel is whole wheat, and try cottage cheese as a topping (I love it with sliced tomato).

Cheeseburger and fries: If there's broiled or roasted chicken or turkey or a veggie burger on the menu, go for that instead and choose a baked potato over fries any day.

Movie popcorn: Hold the butter!

Chicken nuggets: There's not much you can do with these in a restaurant, but at home, you can bake instead of fry them. Just use a little oil spray on the pan and the chicken so they don't dry out as they cook.

Orange juice: Eat an actual orange instead!

If you have any ideas for how to bump up the nutritional value of your favorite foods, I'd love to know about them. You can email them to me at sensationalsubstitutions@girlsonlyweightloss.com.

Fabulous Factor Two: Eat Smaller Portions

"Super size," "extra large," "buy one, get one free," "more for your money"

Everywhere we go we are encouraged to buy and eat larger amounts of food. Restaurants and food markets compete for customers by promising more food at lower prices than the next one is selling. Sounds like a good deal? It isn't! This "bigger is better," "more for your money" way of life is contributing to adults, children, and teenagers becoming fatter now, than they have ever been in history. And they haven't stopped growing (in width, not height!!). For some reason, we don't want to resist a deal, with our bodies paying the price.

I once bought a box of cookies so large that it should have taken my whole family six months to finish it (I couldn't resist, it was on sale!). But, since the cookies were right there, and since there were so many, we all ate cookies every day. The box was empty in two weeks. As you probably realize, we ate far more cookies than our bodies needed to be healthy. And I know I'm not alone. Have you ever ordered the extra-large fries because they're only thirty cents more than the small? Come home with eight boxes of cheese crackers because there was a two-for-one sale? Eaten six pieces of garlic bread because it's free on the table, and then a huge plate of pasta that you ordered? Bought a super size candy bar because you get 25 percent more free? Or chosen the jumbo movie popcorn because you get a free soda? If you answered "yes" to any of the above "good deals" (or if your parents get them for you), you'll find this section very interesting.

Since we are surrounded by huge amounts of food, supersized everything, and supposedly great value for our money, it's easy to lose sight of how much we are actually eating *compared to how much our bodies really need*. In fact, one of the most common ways that teenage girls gain too much weight is by eating more than they think they are eating. This can happen quite easily because when you are faced with a huge amount of food it becomes much easier to ignore what your stomach is telling you and just eat what's in front of you. In other words, you use the portion size, rather than your body's cues, to tell you when to stop eating (check out Chapter 6, Family Pattern #1, for a review of this). You can probably guess that this will lead to you eating much more than you need to be healthy.

Of course it can be difficult to know what a serving (portion) should actually look like. So, Dr. Marshel gave me some great ways to figure it out. I think you'll be as surprised as I was to realize how easy it is to overeat. After you look at the serving sizes, go back to the quiz foods again (in the previous section) and figure out what a serving size of each item would look like.

Surprising Serving Sizes

+ A serving of cooked pasta or rice, fruit salad, cooked cereal or vegetables is about equal to an adult's closed fists held together (about a cup).

+ A serving of a baked potato is about the size of a computer mouse. If your potato is much bigger, cut it in half and only eat the second half if you're still hungry at the end of your meal.

+ A serving of cold cereal is two large handfuls or the size of a pair of loosely rolled up sports socks (about a cup). Try filling your cereal bowl the way you usually do and compare. You may be eating two or three servings at once without even realizing it.

+ A serving of a bagel is the size of a makeup compact. Many bagels are two or three times this size. Consider eating a mini-bagel or half the bagel instead.

+ A serving of butter, margarine, cream cheese or mayonnaise is equal to the tip of your thumb to the first joint. Keep this in mind when you're making sandwiches.

+ A serving of peanut butter is the size of a golf ball.

+ A serving of meat, chicken, turkey or fish is about the size of the palm of a woman's hand or a deck of cards. When you're eating lunch or dinner, eat this amount as your first helping and then think about whether you want more.

+ A serving of a muffin (corn, bran, chocolate chip, etc.) is the size of two large eggs or a softball. Wow, this one shocked me. I could easily eat one of those humongous bakery muffins for a snack. Instead, eat a quarter or a half and split the rest with a friend or save it for tomorrow.

+ A serving of cheese is one string cheese, or it's the size of your whole index finger, or the shape of an index card (American or sliced cheese).

✦ A serving of a waffle or pancake is equal to a CD.

✦ A serving of a burger is the size of the palm of a woman's hand.

✦ A serving of French fries is ten fries (no more supersized fries for me!).

✦ A serving of pizza is one slice.

✦ A serving of chips or pretzel twists is about fourteen.

✦ A serving of ice cream or frozen yogurt is one scoop (about ½ a cup).

✦ A serving of juice or soda is one cup.

If you're not sure what a serving size is for a particular food, you can usually look at the "Nutrition Facts" label on the back of the package. The first item is always Serving Size. For example, the serving size for red licorice is five pieces (not the whole package, which is what I almost ate while writing this chapter!).

There is a big problem with some food labels that really makes me angry. In order to encourage sales, some food manufacturers label their products in a way that makes them look as if they are low-calorie or low-fat, when they really aren't. They do this by *making the serving size unreasonably small.* For example, a bottle of Snapple contains two servings—so you have to double the number of calories and sugar you're getting if you drink the whole bottle—and who buys an individually sized bottle of juice and drinks only half? I've seen the same thing on labels of *individual* size potato chips (a bag contains two servings—would you eat only half a small bag of chips?) and even on a package of muffins (one smallish muffin was two servings!). I think that when manufacturers do this, it is deceitful and shows us that they are only concerned about selling their product—not helping us have healthy eating habits. This means that it is up to you to be an educated buyer and eater—read the labels and don't be fooled!

You may find it difficult to adjust to eating smaller, healthier servings of food. At first, you might feel like you're not eating enough. However, as you get used to looking at food in a less supersized way, you'll become very good at paying attention to whether you are eating because you're hungry or because there's still food in front of you. Here are some tips to help you start:

* Don't supersize anything, even if it's the best deal of the century. Instead get a "small" or "medium" of foods such as burgers, fries, sodas, movie popcorn or ice cream. If you can only get a supersized food, split it with someone or throw the rest away. Remember, healthy eating and feeling good about your body is always the best deal, even if it's not the least expensive.

* When you're eating a meal, put one serving (of each item) on your plate or in your bowl and eat it. When you're done, take a second helping of the same size, only if you're still hungry.

* When you're eating out, estimate servings the same way as you do at home. Get a second plate and put one serving of each food onto that plate and eat until you're full. If you finish it and still want more, take another serving (if doing this makes you feel self-conscious, simply divide the portions up on your plate). Try not to eat more than two servings, even if there's a lot left on the first plate. Ask the waiter to pack it up for you to take home so you won't feel like you wasted it. You can warm it up later, when you're hungry again, or eat it tomorrow.

Terrific Teen Tip: Caitlin (age 16) and her family eat out quite often so Caitlin has become good at looking at her meal and estimating the serving sizes. She always asks for an extra plate with her meal. Then she leaves herself one (or two if she's really starving) servings of food on her plate, immediately putting the rest onto the extra plate. Before she even begins eating, she asks the waiter to put the extra food in a take-out bag. This way she's not even tempted to eat it. Caitlin says this has really helped her become good at sticking to her healthy eating plan. She also looks forward to having another meal the next day from her leftovers.

❈ When you're eating a snack, take one serving size and put it in a bowl, then put the rest away. If you're really hungry, eat a healthy meal instead of the snack because otherwise you may eat five servings of the snack before you're full. Save the snack for later.

Fabulous Factor Three: Eat Enough

First, I tell you to eat smaller portions, now I tell you to eat enough! Factors Two and Three may seem contradictory at first, but actually, they go together very well. Eating smaller portions does not mean you should let yourself be hungry. If you eat too little food, or if you eat foods that don't satisfy your hunger or provide your body with nutrients (like Sweets and Treats) you will find yourself hungry again very quickly. When you let yourself get hungry, you'll be likely to reach for more of the things that seem quickly satisfying, but which don't provide your body with real energy or hunger satisfaction.

You can and should make food choices that don't allow this unhealthy cycle to happen. Follow the tips below to see how you can use Factors Two and Three together to feel satisfied, have energy, and resist the urge to eat junk food all the time.

1. When you eat a meal, make sure your stomach is satisfied. Do this by eating one portion at a time. Stop when you feel content but not full.

2. Tell yourself that when you are hungry, you will eat again—don't lie to yourself by skipping meals or snacks when you are hungry.

3. Carry a healthy snack (e.g., fruit, a sandwich, a granola bar, yogurt) with you. If you become hungry but can't get to a meal (e.g., between classes), eat this snack so you don't get so starved that you grab anything—chips, candy, etc.—without caring if it contains too much fat or is not nutritious.

4. Don't go for more than three or four hours (except when you're sleeping) without eating a serving of something nutritious.

5. Drink water, seltzer, or flavored water whenever you can. Carry a bottle with you everywhere, especially in warm weather and when you're exercising or moving around a lot. Don't replace these with soda (diet or regular) or juice.

Fabulous Factor Four: Eat Foods You Like and Don't Deprive Yourself of Foods You Love

"Kathy (age 14): I had to lose weight so I decided that the best way would be to stop eating all the foods I love—since those are the ones I overeat. I cut out pasta, orange soda, tortilla chips, and peanut butter. But I couldn't stick to it because all I thought about was the foods I was missing. Eventually I gave up and I still haven't lost any weight. I think I've even gained some pounds!"

Kathy teaches us a good lesson: *If you deprive yourself of foods you like, you won't successfully manage your weight or body fat.* This is because your goal is not simply to lose weight or fat, but to learn a whole new approach to managing food, exercise, and your body. *Dr. Susan's Girls-Only Weight Loss Guide* is a lifestyle that you can use forever (even as an adult). But it would fail if I told you that you had to stop eating foods that you love. So, Factor Four is simple—eat foods you like, don't eat foods you hate, and don't stop eating foods you love, even if they are part of the Sweets and Treats category. Nothing is forbidden! When it comes to Sweets and Treats, the key is to eat smaller servings, eat them less frequently and balance them with lots of healthy foods in the Main Menu category.

Sensational Substitutions (Part II)

Sometimes, there is more than one food that can satisfy your craving for a certain flavor texture or taste. Rather than grabbing the first thing that comes to mind, you might be able to find a healthier, less fatty, lower calorie food that will give you *exactly the same satisfaction*. (BUT, if it doesn't satisfy you, *don't make the substitution*. Remember the fat-free cookies, you might eat ten of them but never be satisfied, whereas one serving—one or two—of regular cookies would do the trick. Lots of fat-free cookies—or potato chips, cake, muffins—may contain less fat but not have significantly fewer calories. Rather, eat one serving of what you desire.)

But, in some cases, you will be satisfied with a healthier substitution. For example, take chocolate. You might be in the mood for a whole candy bar. But perhaps three or four chocolate sucking candies, a few pieces of chocolate licorice, a bowl of chocolate cereal with milk, or a small chocolate frozen yogurt would satisfy you too (with much less fat and fewer calories). If you choose the cereal or yogurt, you even get some protein and calcium. But if you think you need the real thing, or if a substitute is nowhere in sight, remember Factor Two and go for half the chocolate bar or a couple of minis instead.

Here are some other substitutions that will satisfy your cravings in a healthier way:

* You're thinking potato chips but maybe it's the crunch and salt you want. Perhaps pretzels, salted air-popped popcorn or a couple of rice cakes would do the trick. Whichever you choose, remember to put one serving in a bowl (don't eat from the bag) and put the rest away.

* You've got your eye on a glazed donut. But perhaps your sweet tooth would be satisfied by a donut hole, a handful of jelly beans, a lollipop or a cup of caramel popcorn.

* A large peanut butter chunk ice-cream cone is calling you but perhaps what you need to hear is a small peanut butter frozen yogurt or sorbet, or simply a smaller scoop of ice cream.

Factor Four definitely suggests choosing foods you like, but it also includes encouraging yourself to try healthy foods that you may think you don't like or don't love at first bite. Did you know that it can take someone five or more trials of a food before they begin to like it? So if you're not a fruit or vegetable lover, it is still your responsibility to your body to keep trying different fruits and vegetables until you find ones you do like. Your body needs the nutrients from these foods to be healthy and you're the only one who can make sure your body gets them.

Myths and Mistakes

The Four Fabulous Factors have taught you a lot about how to become healthier, but there may still be a few small bad habits hanging around. This is because there are many myths about eating that cause girls to eat unhealthily, all the while thinking they're actually making healthy choices. We're going to bust through these myths, so all your choices can be educated, and help you take powerful steps towards a healthier you!

Myth: Eating breakfast just makes you want to eat more, so it's better to skip it.

Fact: If you skip breakfast, you'll be starving later on and you'll be more likely to overeat for the rest of the day. Your best bet is to eat some protein and some healthy carbohydrates at breakfast time. Don't forget a glass of water!

Myth: If you eat the same foods every day, you'll be less likely to "make a mistake" and eat too much or eat the wrong thing.

Fact: You'll go crazy with boredom if you always eat exactly the same thing. Variety is good for you. Just remember the Four Fabulous Factors and you'll be fine.

Myth: When in doubt, eat a large salad for lunch or dinner.

Fact: A salad is a **Largely Liquid** food that won't satisfy you for long unless you add some protein and carbohydrates to it. Try including some tuna, chicken, beans or cheese and a couple of slices of whole-wheat toast to round out your salad.

Myth: If it's "low-fat" or "no-fat" you can eat as much as you want.

Fact: I've said this already—no matter what the label says, the key is portion control.

Myth: If you take a multivitamin every day, you don't have to worry about how you eat.

Fact: Vitamins don't take the place of healthy foods, but they can give you an extra nutritional boost. You need to eat proteins, carbohydrates, and healthy fats every day.

Myth: Frozen coffee drinks are low-calorie or low fat.

Fact: Most of the coffee "coolata," "frappucinno" type drinks are packed with cream and sugar and huge numbers of calories. You're better off with an iced coffee with lots of skim or low fat milk. If you like it sweet, use regular sugar rather than an artificial sweetener (which is full of chemicals). While coffee is not so great for you, at least you're getting some protein in the milk.

Myth: If you become a vegetarian, you will automatically lose weight and become healthier.

Fact: A vegetarian diet can be healthy (we'll discuss this next). But if you take meat and poultry out of your diet and replace them with lots of pasta, candy, cake, and bread instead of good vegetarian sources of protein well . . . you can figure it out.

Vegetarian Vibes

The number of vegetarian teenagers is growing by leaps and bounds! Some preteens and teenagers are choosing a vegetarian lifestyle because they are concerned about animals and the environment, while others are doing it because they feel it's a healthier way to eat (e.g., less saturated fat from meat). Still others are doing it because it seems "cool" or because their friends are into it. Finally, some girls are choosing vegetarian eating because they believe it's a sure way to lose weight. No matter what your reason, you require knowledge in order to make the best decisions for your body. So you need to know that the last reason I gave for some girls becoming a vegetarian—to lose weight—will not work if you don't have the knowledge for how to eat healthily as a vegetarian. And even if you do lose weight, you need to be sure that you're getting all the nutrients we've discussed so far, and that you're not overdoing your weight loss. In other words, as a vegetarian, you still need to follow all the guidelines that I've outlined in this chapter. Furthermore, if you don't truly feel strongly about eating in a vegetarian way, this will be no different than any diet you try—you will feel deprived, and it will fail. Being a vegetarian should not be a weight loss technique, but it might help you lose weight just as any other healthy eating plan would do.

A vegetarian lifestyle can be very healthy (don't let anyone tell you otherwise!) if you do it the right way. In fact, studies have shown that people who rely more on a vegetable-based diet are less likely to become very overweight than those who eat lots of meat. So I spoke with a real expert, and even better, a wonderful woman, Dr. Reed Mangels, a nutritionist who specializes in healthy vegetarian eating. She gave me tons of great information about how girls can be healthy vegetarians (see more about Dr. Mangels as well as some great resources for teen vegetarians at the end of the book).

You may not realize it, but there are several different types of vegetarians. The main ones (although there are other variations too) are:

* Vegans who eat only foods from plants and don't eat anything that came from animals. They avoid meat, fish, poultry, eggs, and dairy

* Lacto-vegetarians who eat plant foods and dairy products, but not meat, fish, poultry or eggs.

* Lacto-ovo-vegetarians who eat plant foods, dairy, and eggs, but not meat, fish or poultry.

* Ovo-vegetarians who eat plant foods and eggs, but not meat, fish, poultry or dairy products.

* Pesco-vegetarians who eat plant foods, dairy, eggs, and fish, but not meat or poultry (I've been a pesco for over twenty years!).

* Semi-vegetarians who eat everything but red meat.

Food for Thought

Dr. Mangels explains that eating healthily as a vegetarian usually requires a little extra thought and meal planning. This is because vegetarians need to be just as concerned as everyone else about getting all the nutrients their bodies need to grow. This can be a little tricky if you don't eat the most available sources of protein—meat, poultry, fish or dairy.

Plant-based foods do contain protein, but the proteins in these foods (including grains and legumes) are incomplete. What does this mean? Here's a quick science lesson. Proteins are made up of amino acids. There are nine different amino acids that your body needs to be healthy. Animal proteins (meat, fish, dairy, eggs) generally supply your body with all nine amino acids. But each type of plant-based food contains only some of the nine (different plant-based foods contain different amino acids). If you include fish, dairy or eggs in your vegetarian diet on a regular basis, you don't have to worry about getting enough complete proteins. But if you don't, you need to make sure you eat *a wide variety* of a variety of plant-based foods, so your body gets all nine of the amino acids. In addition, as a vegetarian, your body continues to require healthy carbohydrates and healthy fats. Dr. Mangels also told me that vegetarian girls who don't eat dairy products need to be sure they get enough calcium, which may be missing in their diets. So if you don't eat dairy products make sure to include a variety of calcium rich foods on a regular basis. She also explained that iron is another important mineral that your body requires, but that could be missing in your diet if you don't eat meat. So it's important to be sure that you are eating iron-rich foods. Last, if you eat a strictly vegan diet, your body could become low in B-12, a vitamin that is very important for producing healthy blood and nerves in your body. This is a lot of information to keep track of, so I've put together a simple table to help you make smart eating vegetarian choices.

The Nutrients a Healthy Vegetarian Teen Needs

Nutrients your body needs	Foods
Protein	Fruits, vegetables, grains, nuts, nut butters, seeds, legumes, soy products (soy milk, soy beans, soy nuts, tofu, miso, tempeh, seitan, veggie burgers, veggie dogs, foods containing TVP—textured vegetable protein)
Carbohydrates	Vegetables, fruits, whole grain breads, whole wheat pasta
Healthy fats	Nuts, nut butters, seeds, soy products, legumes
Calcium	Broccoli, bok choy, kale, collard greens, turnip greens, legumes, soy beans, calcium fortified juices, calcium fortified soy or rice milk
Iron	Legumes, spinach, chard, beet greens, iron-fortified breakfast cereals
Vitamin B-12	Fortified breakfast cereals (read the label), fortified meat substitutes (e.g., veggie nuggets, burgers etc.—read the label to make sure it's fortified), nutritional yeast, fortified soy or rice milk, take a B-12 supplement (speak to your doctor first because your body needs very little B-12 to be healthy)

As you can see in the table, many foods are in more than one category. It is a good idea to eat these foods frequently to ensure that you're getting all the nutrients you need, especially if you don't eat fish, eggs or dairy.

Some foods are easy to prepare and some require a little more effort. There are lots of vegetarian cookbooks; some especially for teens that you can buy or take out of the library (see Appendix 2). Learning how to cook will not only give you a larger variety of vegetarian foods to try, it will also give you greater control over being able to make healthy choices—you won't have to rely on others cooking for you.

If you're thinking of becoming vegetarian (or even semivegetarian), the best way to start is to do it gradually. Make a list of the vegetarian foods that you already eat—you'll probably be surprised that it's more than you think. Then slowly add more vegetables, beans, soy foods, and meat replacements to your diet. Remember, DON'T SIMPLY REPLACE MEAT WITH CHEESE OR CARBOHYDRATES. This won't make you healthier—look for Main Menu sources of protein and eat lots of fruit and vegetables. And don't forget to pay attention to serving sizes—being vegetarian doesn't change that either.

Now that you know how to eat in a healthy way (and hopefully you're already starting to make the changes!), Chapter 9 is going to teach you how to eat the same way when you go out. Some of it you already know (like dividing your plate of food into serving sizes), but the next chapter is going to give you some more tips for eating out, as well as a long list of healthy choices in all your favorite fast food restaurants!

Healthy Eating Anywhere and Everywhere

The Power of Knowledge

Girls often become frustrated when they're trying to eat healthily because they don't know what to do when they're eating in a restaurant, or hanging out with their friends at the mall. For example, it's upsetting and frustrating when you agree to go to a restaurant with your friends, but then you sip diet soda the whole time, feeling too guilty to eat. It's just as frustrating when you eat too much and then feel guilty afterwards. It doesn't have to be this way!

Restaurants, fast food, mall food, and school food (if you dare) can all be a part of your new healthy lifestyle. In fact, you can still lose weight while eating them! Simply pay attention to the Four Fabulous Factors in Chapter 8. Healthy, nutritious eating isn't only about one meal; it's about what you eat over a whole day, a week, a month, and a year. Besides, it is possible to eat everywhere and still be healthy. This chapter will help you to continue feeling healthy and in control while still being able to fit into any eating situation and not feel deprived or left out. You will be able to use this chapter as a guide anytime you eat out. You will find ideas for eating healthily in different situations. It also includes the best food choices for different types of restaurants and an overall guideline for what to avoid when eating out.

The Basics

You would be surprised how easy it is to turn a healthy food into an unhealthy one just by the way it is prepared. Remember tempura from the last chapter—vegetables become greasy blobs of fat when a Japanese restaurant serves them battered and deep fried! There are many food preparations that pack on the calories and fat in a similar way (chicken nuggets, onion rings, nachos). This doesn't mean they should be avoided (remember, *never* deprive yourself), but it is important for you to have knowledge so you can make educated choices. For example, you may decide to eat the tempura or chicken nuggets for lunch and then have a healthier meal for dinner. Or you may decide to split an order of onion rings or nachos with a friend and find that eating just a few pieces will satisfy your craving.

Menus usually have "giveaway" words that describe the way a food is prepared. These words will give you an excellent clue about whether a dish is high in fat and/or calories or whether it is a healthy choice. As long as you know what you're getting, you can make educated decisions. Healthier foods—those prepared without too much added fat or calories—usually have the following words somewhere in the description: *stir-fried, baked, sautéed in olive oil, grilled, broiled, boiled, roasted* or *steamed.*

These are typically **Main Menu** foods. Foods in the **Consider with Caution** category are described with words such as: *fried, deep-fried, extra crispy, sweet and sour, tempura, extra cheese, hollandaise, creamed, bisque, creamy, rich* or *dense.*

If you choose one of these foods, you'll do your body a favor if you eat it as a side dish rather than as your main meal—or better yet, split it with a couple of friends and find a Main Menu food as your main course. Also, you'll be wise to limit the number of Consider with Caution and Sweets and Treats foods you eat at one time. For example, if you know you're going to want an awesome dessert, choose a healthier Main Menu dish for your main course.

Check Out the Menu

I'm going to make it really easy for you to find healthy selections on the menu, no matter the restaurant, snack counter or activity with which you're confronted. Dr. Marshel helped me come up with the healthiest choices in each style of restaurant or place you want to eat. So all you need to do is choose your meal or snack using the types of foods I've provided, and you'll find yourself eating as healthily as possible. When in doubt, refer back to the list of healthy preparations listed above—you might even want to write them on a little card to keep in your wallet. Also, don't forget to pay attention to serving sizes. Also, stick to water, seltzer or unsweetened iced tea!

Pizza (Your hangout or a fast-food pizza place, like Bertucci's, California Pizza Kitchen, Chuck E. Cheese's, Domino's, Godfather's, Hot Stuff Pizza, Little Caesars, Pappa John's, Pizza Hut, Pizza Pro, Round Table Pizza, Sbarro, Shakey's)

➡ Go for the regular or thin crust type.

➡ Veggie, ham, and chicken toppings are awesome, but stay away from stuffed crusts, extra cheese, beef, pepperoni, and sausage.

➡ Nix any pizza that has the word "big," "extreme," "extra large," or "supreme" in its title!

⇒ Limit the number of bread sticks and garlic knots you eat, even though they are really tempting.

⇒ Don't forget to use your stomach (not your eyes) to tell you how many slices you eat (one slice equals a serving).

Burgers and such (Burger King, Carl's Jr., Hardee's, Jack-in-the-Box, McDonalds, Sonic, Wendy's, and all the others)

⇒ Begin by NOT choosing burgers, sandwiches, fries or other foods whose names contain the following words: Super, Supreme, Big, Jumbo, Double, Ultimate, Extreme, Deluxe, Monster or Large (did I leave any out?). Instead choose items that are Small or Medium—simple right!

⇒ Next, unless you really love it, request your burgers without mayonnaise or any kind of "special sauce"—which always contains mayonnaise! Instead use ketchup or mustard for flavor.

⇒ When you order a salad, request low-fat or nonfat dressing or use just a little bit of the regular dressing.

⇒ Milk shakes, thick shakes, or ice-cream shakes usually have as many calories and fat as a whole meal. If you've just got to have one, get it as dessert with an extra cup or two, and split it with a couple of friends.

⇒ Most burger restaurants now have healthy-choice or "light" sections on their menus that make choosing your meal easier. These usually include salads (don't forget the protein) and healthier sandwiches.

⇒ Fast-food breakfasts aren't the most fabulous. But if you find yourself there, your best choices are egg sandwiches—you'll get some good protein with carbohydrates to fuel your energy supply for the day. Hash browns are okay too, and so are hotcakes if you don't drown them in butter or syrup! You're better off without sausage, bacon, or biscuits, which tend to be higher in calories and fat and not as filling or nutritious.

Hot dogs (Any hot dog stand or a place like Nathan's Famous, Uncle Al's Hot Dogs, or Wienerschnitzel)

→ If you can find a low-fat hot dog, go for it.

→ Some hot dog restaurants also have food other than hot dogs (for example, subs, sandwiches or salads), which may be healthier. You'll have to use your best judgment! If not, it's all about portion sizes. For example, choose a regular hot dog, rather than an extra-long and stick with small fries. Overall, hot dogs are not amongst the world's healthiest foods—they're packed with artificial flavors, colors, and preservatives. So choose to eat them (at home or out) only once in a while.

Chicken (Boston Market, Chick-fil-a, Church's Chicken, Kentucky Fried Chicken, Popeye's, or the place near your home)

→ Your best bet at chicken restaurants (in fact, anywhere you eat chicken) is to order skinless chicken breasts whenever possible, or remove the skin yourself. Skinless chicken is one of the healthiest, highest protein foods you can eat, especially when you order it *broiled, roasted*, or *grilled*. But when chicken is fried (especially extra crispy) or covered with rich sauces it suddenly becomes much less healthy.

→ Popcorn chicken and fried chicken nuggets (small pieces of fried chicken) are even less healthy because you get less protein and more fat in each mouthful. So choose your chicken carefully and you'll have an awesome healthy meal.

→ As always, say "No" to mayonnaise or other creamy spreads on chicken sandwiches.

Fish and seafood (Any seafood restaurant or a chain like Arthur Treacher's, Captain D's, Long John Silvers, Red Lobster)

→ When eating fish or seafood, your best bet is to look for broiled or grilled foods and limit fried or battered fish and other seafood.

→ Choose baked potatoes, corn or greens over French fries, and go for a garden salad.

→ When you're having a sandwich, season it with mustard or ketchup, rather than mayonnaise.

→ As with chicken, don't choose popcorn shrimp or fish or fried or battered fish nuggets, fingers or pieces.

Subs and sandwiches (Your corner delicatessen or a chain such as Au Bon Pain, Blimpie, Quiznos Sub, Subway)

Portion size can be a big issue when it comes to subs. Half a subway sandwich (6") is a much more reasonable (and still filling) meal than a whole one (foot long). Some restaurants have a special healthy choices menu, but if yours doesn't make sure you:

→ Ask for lots of lettuce, tomato, and any other fresh veggies they have.

→ Don't load up on mayonnaise or creamy dressings. For flavor use mustard or ketchup.

→ Choose lean meats such as chicken and turkey.

→ When possible go for a wheat, rather than a white roll.

→ Some sandwich restaurants also serve wraps—the new "in" sandwich. Like other sandwiches, wraps can be healthy or not, depending on how they are prepared. Apply the same rules that you use for all other sandwiches, when deciding what you want in your wrap.

Italian (One of the Italian restaurants in your neighborhood or a chain like Olive Garden or Sbarro)

→ Start with vegetable, minestrone or lentil soups, fresh mozzarella with tomato (not fried mozzarella sticks), a stuffed artichoke or a regular salad.

→ Next go for steamed mussels or clams, chicken marinara, veal marsala, veal chops, pasta primavera (no cream sauce), pasta with clam sauce (red or white), pasta fra diablo, fish of the day (broiled or sautéed) or cheese ravioli with marinara sauce (not cream sauce).

→ If you're really stuck for a choice, a simple bowl of spaghetti and tomato sauce will hit the spot.

→ Portions still count for all of these!

Chinese: (Your local Chinese restaurant or chains like Manchu Wok and Panda Express)

→ First try steamed vegetable or chicken dumplings, hot and sour, wonton or egg-drop soup.

→ Then have chicken or fish with Chinese vegetables, chicken or beef with broccoli or mushrooms, chicken or vegetable chow mein, or beef with black bean sauce.

→ Avoid fried food.

→ Ask for brown rice rather than white rice.

→ Don't forget your serving sizes!

Japanese: (Your favorite Japanese restaurant or one like Benihana)

→ Miso or vegetable soup is a great start, as is edamame (Japanese soy beans) or steamed dumplings.

➡ Then have sushi, sashimi (some people are concerned about eating raw fish, so ask your parents first), teriyaki or sukiyaki.

➡ If you eat sushi, remember that the rice is include in your sushi rolls, so don't eat any extra.

➡ Japanese green tea is really healthy for your body!

Diners and family restaurants: (Your family's favorite or a chain like Applebee's, Chili's Grill and Bar, Denny's, Friendly's, IHOP, Perkins, Sizzler, Steak 'N Shake or T.G.I. Friday's)

➡ In a regular diner, choose scrambled eggs or an omelet (add any veggies you like for extra nutrition) with lettuce and tomato instead of fries or hash browns. Grilled chicken or fish are also good choices, as is a large salad topped with chicken, other lean meat or tuna (no mayo). Try not to choose a meal that is fried (like chicken fingers).

➡ Some of the family-style restaurants have a "low-fat," "low carb," or healthier eating section, which is usually a good place to start as long as you can find good Main Menu items.

➡ Also, ask about the ingredients in a dish and then request that creamy sauces, sour cream, and mayonnaise be served on the side. You can also get burgers or veggie burgers without the cheese.

➡ In family-style restaurants many menu items rely on deep-fried foods (e.g., mozzarella sticks, chicken fingers) and melted cheese (potato skins, nachos). Don't be tempted by these, especially if there are other, just as delicious but healthier items on the menu. Refer to "The Basics" section of this chapter for the key words to look for in foods cooked more healthily.

➡ Ask for fish or chicken to be broiled or grilled and for vegetables to be steamed.

→ Some family-style restaurants have large salad bars. Be sure to check out the "Salad and dessert bar" section of this chapter to help you make healthy choices when eating a salad bar meal.

→ Desserts in some family style restaurants are usually unbelievably scrumptious, but one dessert can have more calories than a whole day's worth of food. So share, share, share!

Steakhouses (Like Bonanza, Steak and Ale, Golden Corral, Outback Steakhouse or Ponderosa)

→ Ask the waiter to recommend the leanest steak possible.

→ Choose an eight-ounce steak, rather than larger.

→ You might even consider broiled or grilled chicken or fish, if they're on the menu.

→ Choose steamed veggies such as carrots, broccoli or spinach and a baked potato or rice as side dishes (rather than fries or mashed potato).

→ Go for a salad too, with a splash of oil and vinegar or a low-fat or light salad dressing, rather than a creamy topping. (See the Salad and dessert bar section for more on salads.)

Sandwich/soup/salad/stuffed potato restaurants (Like Au Bon Pain, The Great Steak and Potato Company or Tim Horton's)

→ Pick sandwiches the way you would in a deli—lean meats and poultry with lettuce and tomato and little or no mayonnaise (light mayonnaise if they have it).

→ When possible choose whole grain breads, bagels, and rolls, rather than white bread.

→ Soup can be packed with great nutrition if you choose right. Go for bean, vegetable, mushroom barley or pea soup.

→ Salads, as always should be heavy on the fresh veggies and light on everything else including creamy dressings.

→ To make your salad a meal, add grilled chicken or a scoop of tuna (no mayo or light mayo).

Delicatessen: Deli food is great for lunch or dinner on the run. Some girls even hit the deli for breakfast. So here are some tips to make sure your deli experience satisfies your appetite as well as your nutritional needs.

→ If you're a deli breakfaster, choose foods that give you protein as well as some (but not too many) carbohydrates. For example, instead of a bagel and cream cheese, choose a scrambled egg on whole-wheat toast.

→ If you really want one of those massive muffins, cut it in half and share it with a friend.

→ Low-fat milk or orange juice is a better choice than coffee. However, decaf coffee that is about half low-fat or skim milk (in France this is called café au lait) isn't too bad. Tea is also a good choice, with less caffeine than coffee.

→ For lunch or dinner, chicken breast, sliced turkey, ham, or roast beef sandwiches are all great—especially on whole wheat bread (mustard or ketchup instead of mayo).

→ If you're not into the meat thing, cheese, tuna or egg salad sandwiches—with low-fat or fat-free mayo, if possible, will hit the spot. Some delis also make an awesome Greek salad.

Mexican (The Mexican restaurant you love best or a chain like Del Taco, Taco Bell, Taco Cabana, Taco John's or Taco Time)

→ Start with guacamole, ceviche or black bean soup.

→ Next try a fajita; chicken, bean, or beef taco; chicken, bean or beef burrito; chicken, bean or beef enchilada; or chile con carne.

➡ Mexican food usually comes with healthy black beans and rice.

➡ It's a good idea to avoid the huge, fried tortilla shells that are often used for serving salad—these are a great way to magically transform a healthy salad into something that is anything but healthy.

➡ Control yourself around the chip basket. Have a few, then ask the waiter to take them away—out of sight, out of mind.

➡ Many Mexican dishes arrive swamped in melted cheese and sour cream. You'll do yourself a favor if you ask to have your meal prepared with only a little cheese and with the sour cream on the side.

Greek/Middle Eastern (some of my all-time favorite food)

➡ Begin with yogurt and cucumber, avgolemono (lemon) or bean soup. Other good starters are babaganoush (eggplant spread), yogurt and cucumber salad, hummus (chickpea spread), and pita bread or dolma (stuffed grape leaves).

➡ For a main course choose a Greek salad (with or without grilled chicken), shish kebab, a chicken gyro or souvlaki or broiled fish.

➡ Tabouli, couscous (both grains) or rice make a good side dish.

Salad and dessert bars: (These can be found in many restaurants and even in some supermarkets)

➡ At a standard restaurant or supermarket salad bar, go for any vegetables and greens that are freshly cut and NOT in a dressing.

➡ Then add low-fat cottage cheese (don't assume it is low-fat), eggs, garbanzo beans (chickpeas), sunflower seeds, and low-fat or fat-free dressing.

➡ A sprinkling of cheese is also fine.

➡ You could also add tuna (no mayo) and a whole wheat bread roll, for a super-healthy, well-rounded meal.

→ At all you can eat salad bars in restaurants, start with fresh vegetables and fruits. Then add items that aren't deep-fried, or swimming in creamy or greasy sauces. Try your best to find Main Menu foods. If it's not easy to find these foods, then do your best to eat healthily by controlling your portions.

→ Stick with lower fat salad dressings.

→ Soups are often a great choice at a buffet. Hearty chicken, vegetable, mushroom or bean soups are delicious and feed your body's needs as well.

→ Portion control counts for salad bar desserts, too! Just because there are six different desserts offered on the buffet, it doesn't mean you should eat them all. If you want to try more than one, eat just a little of each.

Bagel shops (Your local bagel store or a chain, such as Bruegger's Bagel Bakery)

→ Order whole wheat or other grainy bagels whenever you can.

→ Many bagel stores make enormous bagels that equal two or more servings each. In this case, order a mini-bagel or ask to have the inside of your bagel scooped out, or eat half and save the rest for later (remember the serving sizes in Chapter 7).

→ When it comes to toppings, use a very thin layer of cream cheese (light, if possible), or even better, top your bagel with something nutritious such as egg or tuna salad (request low-fat mayo whenever possible), lean turkey, ham, chicken breast, or a scrambled egg.

→ If you are given a huge amount of topping, take some off. If you like, ask for a container so you can take it home for you or someone else to eat later.

→ Stores that sell bagels often also sell croissants, delicious looking muffins, and other baked goods. These are generally a less healthy choice than a grainy bagel topped with a healthy topping.

They are also usually much larger than a serving size. So, if you must have something sweet, share it or eat half and save the rest for later.

Coffee shops (Starbucks, Dunkin Donuts, and others)

➡ Large, creamy, chocolaty or malted drinks at coffee shops can be very tempting! But, like thick shakes each one can be packed with calories and fat. So beware of these desserts disguised as coffee!

➡ Instead, try a latte or iced coffee made with skim or low-fat milk. Along with the coffee you'll get some protein and calcium from the milk. A spoon or two of sugar won't harm you.

➡ Flavored coffees can add a yummy, satisfying flavor.

Ice cream, frozen yogurt, and smoothie shops (Like Baskin-Robbins, Carvel, Dairy Queen, Freshens, Haagen Daz or TCBY)

➡ Choose soft-serve ice cream or frozen yogurt over hard ice cream.

➡ Sorbet, ices, and sherbet are also great choices, and especially refreshing on a hot summer day.

➡ "Premium" ice creams tend to have the highest amount of fat and calories of all. This is because the premium ingredient is cream rather than milk. Premium ice cream is also denser, rather than being pumped with air.

➡ Add a nutritious nut topping, rather than candy or crushed cookies.

➡ Choose a cup or a wafer cone, rather than a sugar cone (especially those huge ones coated with chocolate!).

➡ Smoothies made with only juices, low-fat/skim milk, real fruit, and ice are a great alternative to shakes, which should almost always be your last choice.

→ Portion control is the key when it comes to frozen treats. Go for a small every time.

Donuts and cookies (e.g., Dunkin Donuts, Krispy Kreme, Mrs. Fields)

→ Let's face it, there is no real nutritional value in donuts and cookies. But, if you want something sweet, don't deprive yourself—you've read enough of this book to know that depriving yourself will only lead to a binge sometime later. Instead, eat the food your mouth desires. When it comes to sweets it's all about *portion control* so just don't eat too much.

→ Some cookies and donuts have fewer calories and less fat than others, so don't be afraid to ask for the nutritional information so you can make an educated choice.

→ Beware of humongous muffins, crullers, and danishes. A donut, two or three donut holes, or a cookie is almost always a better choice.

Convenience stores (Local 24-hour corner shop or a chain like 7-11 or Circle K)

→ For a late night craving, rip open a bag of pretzels, popcorn or baked potato chips, rather than nachos or fried chips, and stick to a single serving size.

→ If you seek something cold, a small slushy, plain fudge bar or fruit juice bar will hit the spot. Beware of those "premium" ice creams that come individually packaged in a box!

→ Decaffeinated coffee or tea with low-fat or skim milk will warm you up on the way to school.

→ Don't be tempted by the hot dogs (how long have they been sitting there anyway?) or microwaveable sandwiches—who knows what's in them.

➡ Some convenience stores carry really healthy stuff like fruit, packaged salad and yogurt.

➡ Resist chocolate milk or chocolate drinks (unless they are low fat) and opt instead for flavored water.

Vending

➡ Pop in your coins and select pretzels, popcorn, baked potato chips, trail mix, nuts, raisins, sunflower seeds, a granola bar, cereal bar, wheat crackers, a mini-cereal box, a fig bar (Fig Newton) or a bag of mini-graham crackers.

School

➡ Choose a sandwich (turkey, chicken, tuna, egg salad) or meat or pasta with tomato sauce or marinara topping.

➡ For dessert, go for fruit, Jello, or pudding.

➡ If your school really scores an "F" when it comes to healthy lunches, you're probably better off brown bagging it or going off campus if you're allowed to leave during the day.

Parties

➡ Like everywhere else, it's all about portion control. Don't get carried away by the partying, group atmosphere. Having fun doesn't mean you have to eat two extra slices of pizza. Rather, eat slowly, listen to your body's signals and when you're done eating, STOP. Being with your friends is the really fun part.

➡ Don't hang out next to the bowl of nachos or candy. Take a handful on a plate or in a cup and find somewhere else to socialize.

➡ When there is a choice of snacks, pick pretzels, baked potato chips, dried fruit, nuts, and veggies.

By now you have all the information you need about eating healthily, which means that you're ready to take the next step. But, believe it or not, it is possible take the quest for health too far. Teenage girls can easily become at risk for developing eating disorders. Since eating disorders are very serious and can even be tragic, let's take a little time in the next chapter to learn about them and make sure that you aren't heading in the direction having one.

Ten

Understanding Eating Disorders (and Getting Help)

When Healthy Eating Gets Off Track

Most girls laugh when I suggest that under certain circumstances, the desire to become thinner could result in an eating disorder. "It's impossible," they say. "I have a hard enough time trying to limit my eating. You don't have to worry that I'll stop eating." In fact some girls have told me they secretly wish they could "get anorexia for just a little while" so they would have the willpower to eat less and lose some weight. When I hear this, I explain that eating disorders don't work this way and that you can't turn them on and off as you like. Furthermore, as you will discover, the very, very serious health problems associated with eating disorders can result in hospitalizations, lifelong struggles with food and weight, and even death.

You've probably heard and read a lot about the two most talked about eating disorders, anorexia and bulimia. You may even know someone who has one of these illnesses. But these aren't the only eating disorders. The others, which you may not have heard about are bulimarexia, compulsive exercising, binge eating, and compulsive overeating.

One of the most crucial things you need to know about all these eating disorders is that *the sooner you recognize that you have one and then get help, the greater the chance that you will be okay*. It is therefore critical for you to read and think about the following information. If you recognize yourself, even slightly, in any of the descriptions, you must immediately tell an adult whom you trust. If you're nervous to speak directly to an adult, ask a friend to help you. In Appendix 2, I have also included contact information for organizations where you can get information and appropriate help.

How Does an Eating Disorder Begin

Eating disorders often begin as an attempt to lose weight. If you go on a diet, restrict your eating significantly, or place too many demands on yourself to lose weight quickly, you could find yourself struggling with an eating disorder. What's more, if you pressure yourself to achieve a certain weight, shape or perfect look, you are also placing yourself at risk for developing one of the eating disorders I will discuss in this chapter.

Girls are much more likely than boys to develop eating disorders (probably because of society's pressure to be thin). The preteen and teenage years are when eating disorders usually begin. As you know firsthand, being a teenager is confusing and stressful. So many things seem to be out of your control. Your body is changing in ways you'd never imagined. You are confronted with many new choices including how to juggle school and a social life as well as decisions about sex, alcohol, and drugs. It seems your parents, who used to take care of everything for you, now seem to be from a different planet. For some girls, the stresses related to decision making and sudden independence, lead to the intense desire to be in control of *something*. That "something" they choose is eating. However, as you will learn, eating disorders are not something you can control. Before you know it, the eating disorder is controlling you.

In order to recognize whether you (or anyone you care about) are at risk for developing an eating disorder, you need to fully understand the signs and symptoms of each one. Luckily, we have the expertise of a doctor who specializes in treating eating disorders. His name his Dr. Sacker and he shared with me all the information you will need, to understand eating disorders and how to protect yourself from developing one.

Anorexia Nervosa

Anorexia nervosa (or just anorexia) is self-starvation along with an enormous fear of fat as well as seeing yourself as much heavier than you really are. It often begins when a girl decides to go on a diet and then she continues dieting way past the point where she's reached a healthy weight. Dr. Sacker explained that this sometimes happens because the girl convinces herself that she will only be successful and happy if she becomes thin enough.

For some girls, becoming anorexic may also be related to other, significant emotional issues. For example, the disorder may give her attention she feels she's never received from her parents. Food and weight may also be easier to focus on than some other very serious or traumatic concerns in her life (e.g., her parents' divorce, or the fact that she was raped or abused).

All through this book, we have discussed the importance of having realistic expectations for yourself; how losing weight or becoming healthier won't make you more popular, prettier, smarter or more athletic. It also won't solve the other problems in your life. But anorexic girls, or those at risk for anorexia, don't believe this. They feel so strongly that being thin will improve their lives dramatically, that they practically stop eating altogether. Eventually they *can't stop or control themselves*. Even if they want to start eating normally again, they can't get themselves to do it, so they keep getting thinner and thinner. Without help (and sometimes even with it) they may have to be hospitalized.

Dr. Sacker told me that up to 15 percent of anorexic people eventually die of anorexia—that's fifteen out of every one hundred anorexic girls.

As you can imagine, there are significant dangers that come with starvation. If you deprive your body of food on a regular basis you may develop stomach cramps, become weak, and faint, and have difficulty concentrating or studying. But that's just the beginning. There are also scary changes that happen to your body if you become too thin. Your period stops, your breasts become disfigured, your palms can turn orange, and you may start to grow fine hair all over your body, including your hands and face. At the same time, you may lose your eyelash hair, and the hair on your head may start falling out. You can also develop serious heart, kidney, and liver damage, any one of which can kill you.

The bottom line is this: *Anorexia is a serious disorder from which recovery is extremely difficult.* The key to helping someone with signs of anorexia is to make sure they see a doctor as soon as possible. Think about how anorexia can devastate your body and life before you allow yourself to become vulnerable.

The Signs

How can you tell if you (or a friend) may have or be developing anorexia? While you can't know for sure, and a medical diagnosis is extremely important, check the list of symptoms and behaviors below. If any of them are present, consider getting help immediately (for yourself or your friend).

- ✔ Eating very little, dieting strictly or refusing to eat for long periods
- ✔ Constantly thinking about how many calories are in everything you eat
- ✔ Thinking you're fat no matter what you actually look like or what other people tell you
- ✔ Pretending you're not hungry, or convincing yourself you're not, even when you're starving

✔ Telling lies about eating (for example, you tell your mom you've eaten, even when you haven't)

✔ Pretending to eat by moving the food around the plate a lot

✔ Taking laxatives, diet pills or diuretics

✔ Exercising for hours a day

✔ Avoiding being with friends because you don't want to be around social eating

Bulimia

Like anorexia, bulimia also begins with the desire to take control and ends with a complete loss of control. Dr. Sacker explained that sometimes a girl feels jealous of thin people who seem to be able to eat whatever they want without gaining weight. I know many girls have felt exactly like this at one time or another in their lives. Sometimes a girl becomes very frustrated about having to deprive herself (especially if she's put herself on a restrictive diet). Bulimia begins from that wish that she could eat anything she wants and still be thin. Dr. Sacker says that the first step towards bulimia is when the girl decides to eat a very large amount of food all at once (bingeing). But after eating it, she feels guilty and forces herself to throw up (purging) to try and get rid of what she ate. At first this seems like a great plan—you can eat anything you want and then just get rid of it. However, it's not this simple.

First of all, purging is habit forming—you actually get hooked on it. In fact, the bingeing can become a means to get to the purging. A bulimic girl could find herself purging many times in one day. Her whole life becomes controlled by the bingeing and purging. Some bulimic girls also purge using laxatives (pills swallowed, which increase your bowel movements, leading to diarrhea) as another method of getting rid of the food they eat. Others use diuretics ("water pills," which make you urinate). If abused, both of these will damage your body, sometimes permanently.

A bulimic girl will frequently stop hanging out with friends, lie to her family, or steal money to buy binge foods. The control she wanted over her weight vanishes completely and she becomes trapped in the world of bingeing and purging. What's more, a bulimic girl may actually gain weight at times. Even though she purges, her body still absorbs some food from the binge. Her metabolism slows down as her body's response to the bingeing and purging. This then causes weight gain. You don't have to be thin to be bulimic. *A girl can be any weight and still be bulimic.*

The frequent bingeing and purging will have scary effects on a girl's body. Dr. Sacker explained that the vomiting can seriously damage your esophagus (the tube that takes food to your stomach), causing terrible pain and even causing it to rupture. A bulimic's teeth can become black, rotten, and even fall out because the acid from vomit corrodes their teeth. Ulcers (very painful, sometimes bleeding sores—similar to a canker sore) in the digestive tract are also a possible symptom that a bulimic is abusing her body. Frequent bingeing and purging can also affect your heart, causing it to begin beating irregularly. This, Dr. Sacker pointed out, can kill you.

The Signs

As with any other eating disorder, if you recognize yourself (or a friend) in any of the behaviors or symptoms below, seek help immediately because you may have or be developing bulimia.

- ✔ Eating large amounts of food in a very short time (bingeing)
- ✔ Eating or bingeing secretly
- ✔ Throwing up (purging) after eating a meal or a binge
- ✔ Taking diet pills, laxatives or diuretics
- ✔ Becoming scared that you can't stop the bingeing and purging (vomiting, pills)
- ✔ Always feeling guilty about eating
- ✔ Starving yourself between binges

✔ Exercising too much

✔ Stealing food or money to buy food

Bulimarexia

Dr. Sacker told me about another eating disorder, bulimarexia, which is exactly what it sounds like—a combination of anorexia and bulimia. This is when a girl starves herself and is very thin, like an anorexic, and also sometimes binges and purges, like a bulimic. She will have symptoms and behaviors from both disorders.

Compulsive Exercising

Some girls use exercise as a way to control their weight in addition to, or instead of, starvation or purging. They will spend hours a day or a week exercising far beyond the point that is healthy. Often they will justify eating a little "extra" food by then exercising like crazy to "burn it off." This is called compulsive exercising and it can be just as serious as starving or purging. If you are exercising more than anything else, if you've withdrawn from other activities in order to exercise, or if you seem to arrange your life around exercise, you need to acknowledge to yourself that you need help.

Compulsive Overeating

Have you ever sat down and eaten a huge amount of food (much more than most people eat at a meal) in a short period of time, while feeling out of control? Many people have done this at one time or another. But if you do it very often, you might have an eating disorder called compulsive overeating, or binge eating disorder. This is when you eat large amounts of foods, (often secretly like bulimics), but you don't purge (vomit or take pills). Compulsive overeaters sometimes skip meals or "fast" for short periods of time, but then when they become hungry they binge and feel very guilty afterwards. Compulsive overeating is a cycle of eating and guilt. It can be very difficult to break this cycle. Very often, compulsive overeaters eat for reasons other than hunger—they may be sad, angry, frustrated, lonely or scared. Compulsive overeaters stuff down their bad feelings with food so they don't have to feel or think about them.

Sometimes compulsive overeaters think that because they are not super thin and not throwing up, that they don't really have a problem. However, frequent overeating will lead to a girl becoming very overweight, which is just as serious as being too thin. When your body carries too much weight it puts extra stress on your heart, joints, bones, and muscles. As you know from reading this book, being overweight can cause many, many problems with physical and emotional health.

Furthermore, the emotional cycle of bingeing and feeling guilty is also unhealthy. The secrecy can pull you away from family and friends and the need to eat can trap you, making you want to avoid all activities that don't include the chance to eat. This is not a way for anyone to live. So, as with the other eating disorders, please get help.

Getting Help

The first step is admitting to yourself that you have a problem and that you need help. Next, you need to tell an adult you trust. This doesn't have to be your parent. You can speak to your doctor, a teacher, school counselor, school nurse, coach, aunt, grandmother, older sister, or cousin. If it's hard to do it in person, you can write a letter, send an email or even give the adult this chapter to read with the relevant parts marked. If this is too difficult, you can tell a friend and ask her to tell an adult for you. If even this is too painful, there are hotlines and organizations where you can get information and ask for help. At the end of the book, in Appendix 2, is a section called *Eating Disorders* where you can find this information.

The next step is to actually go for help, which may be the most difficult part. Sometimes, when a girl has an eating disorder, she can't admit it to anyone else. In fact, sometimes she really doesn't believe there is anything wrong with her. So, if any of the descriptions above seem familiar to you or if people are telling you you're too thin or that you need help, pay attention—even if you think you're fine. *When it comes to eating disorders, you're often not the best judge of whether you need help.* But if you wait too long it could be too late—remember, eating disorders can kill you!

Helping a Friend

Perhaps the information in this chapter has made you realize that one of your friends may have an eating disorder. Since eating disorders are common among teenage girls, this wouldn't be surprising (in fact, eating disorders are on the rise among teenage boys, too, so it may even be a guy friend you're worried about). But what are you supposed to do? Mind your own business? Confront her? Tell her parent? Tell a school counselor?

I know I've said this already, but it's so important that it bears repeating: *The sooner a person with an eating disorder gets help, the greater their chance of recovery*. This means that if you are worried about your friend, you shouldn't just mind your own business and hope that someone else figures it out. People with eating disorders are very good at hiding the fact that they are starving themselves or bingeing and purging. So perhaps no one else has noticed, or perhaps your friend confided solely in you.

The way you help a friend deal with an eating disorder is no different than how you'd help a friend with alcohol or drugs. If your friend was abusing drugs or you felt she was becoming an alcoholic, would you keep it to yourself? Hopefully not, because the only way she can get help is if a responsible adult knows she has a problem. It's no different with eating disorders. So, if you're worried about a friend, I suggest you do the following:

1. Speak to your friend directly, one-on-one. Try and be as specific as possible about what you're observing. For example, you might say: "I've heard you throwing up in the school bathroom everyday for the past two weeks" or "I've noticed that you never eat lunch any more." She may be relieved that you know and agree to tell an adult. However, there is a good chance that she will deny any problem or that she will become angry with you for suggesting as much. In fact, she may become so angry that she doesn't want to talk to you anymore. It is very common for a person with an eating disorder to deny it one for a long, long time. You shouldn't give in to this denial, no matter how bad you feel.

2. Speak to one or more responsible adults (her parent, a school nurse or counselor) about your concerns. Try and be specific about what you are observing, and why you are worried. This will make the adult take you seriously and will lessen the chances that your concerns will be ignored. If you are worried that your friend will see this as a betrayal, you can ask that your friend not be told that it came from you. In some cases, a counselor will be more likely to respect this confidence than your friend's parent, so take some time to consider who you want to talk to about your friend.

Once you have taken these two steps, THERE IS NOTHING ELSE YOU CAN DO to get help for her. However, as a friend you can comfort and support her if she will allow this. It is not your job to cure your friend, nor is it your job to make sure she gets help. It is not even your job to make sure the adults get help for her. Hopefully, once you've given the information to enough adults, they will get help for her. But even if they don't, you should not feel guilty. You've done your best and there's nothing more you can do.

If your friend is suffering from an eating disorder, you may find that the friendship changes. The focus of her life may be around food, dieting, body weight, and exercising. Dr. Sacker suggests that you not allow yourself to become pulled into this with her. If she wants to talk about food and dieting, change the subject; if she wants you to exercise with her excessively, you should refuse. These things are not good for her and they're not good for you either. You may find that the eating disorder actually ends the friendship. This will be sad for you, but it is not because you're not a good enough friend. Rather, as we've discussed, the eating disorder can take over her life, making it difficult for her to keep up with friendships at that time. But no matter what happens, remember that some day she will (hopefully) be grateful that you tried to help her.

Now, we're ready to move to the next important area—exercise. So, let's jump right in and learn—wait, don't stop reading! You're going to do great! I just KNOW you are—I'm with you all the way.

Believe It or Not,
Exercise Can Be Easy

Why You Need to Get Moving

Wow, you're ten chapters into feeling and looking healthier. Now, here you are at the chapter about moving your body. I'm sure for many of you the thought of exercising is as much fun as stubbing your toe or getting a bad haircut. You'd like to be absent when the gym teacher tells you to run around the track, and you'd do anything to avoid being a fourth in a doubles tennis game. But exercise doesn't have to be a demoralizing, breath sucking, embarrassing experience. If that is how it's been for you then you've been exercising the wrong way or with the wrong people. But I'm *not* saying that you don't have to move your body at all—YOU DO! Exercise will help you feel and look healthier.

Test your knowledge of how exercise can benefit you. Answer True or False to the following statements, then check your answers below (if it isn't your book, use separate paper).

Exercise education:

1. Exercise strengthens your heart.

    TRUE   FALSE

2. If you don't sweat, it isn't a good workout.

    TRUE   FALSE

3. People who exercise need to eat more food than those who don't exercise.

    TRUE   FALSE

4. If you feel your heart pounding during or after exercise, something is wrong.

    TRUE   FALSE

5. You must exercise for hours everyday to get a great body.

    TRUE   FALSE

6. Exercising can affect your mood.

    TRUE   FALSE

7. If your body aches after exercise, you shouldn't do it.

    TRUE   FALSE

8. If you're having fun, you're not getting a great workout.

    TRUE   FALSE

9. Exercise is good for your bones.

    TRUE   FALSE

10. Exercising makes you less hungry.

    TRUE   FALSE

11. If you exercise, you will definitely lose weight.

    TRUE   FALSE

12. It's difficult to lose weight and keep it off without exercising.

    TRUE   FALSE

13. It takes lots of time away from other things to get a good workout.

    TRUE   FALSE

14. Thin girls don't have to exercise.

    TRUE   FALSE

15. You don't have to exercise if you watch what you eat.

    TRUE   FALSE

16. If you exercise, you can eat whatever you want and not gain weight.

    TRUE   FALSE

Scoring: Using the scoring key below, give yourself one point for every correct response and check the explanations to get the exercise education you may be missing.

1. True. Your heart is a muscle that needs to be strengthened just like other muscles. Exercise gets your heart pumping strongly, giving it the workout it needs.

2. False. Some people sweat a lot and some hardly at all, so sweating is not necessarily an indicator of whether you're moving enough. If you incorporate small amounts of movement throughout the day, you might not sweat, but you'll still become healthier. If you exercise hard for more than ten or fifteen minutes, you probably will sweat. Some girls love to sweat! It makes them feel pumped up and healthy.

3. True. Exercise uses the food you eat (and body fat) for energy. So after a good workout or a very active day, you may be hungry. If

so, have a healthy meal to resupply your body's energy. Resist junk food that might give you a quick boost, but won't satisfy your need for nutrition.

4. **Usually False.** When you exercise hard for more than a few minutes, you should expect your heart to pump harder and faster. BUT if your chest hurts or if you feel nauseous, dizzy or breathless, slow down, stop, and make sure you tell your parent and doctor. If you don't usually exercise, it may just be your body adjusting. But just to be sure nothing is wrong, don't ignore these feelings.

5. **False.** As you recall from Chapters 2 and 3, your body shape is determined by puberty and genetics. Exercise can help you become the healthiest feeling and looking person you can be, but it can't magically transform you—not matter how long you work out. It's not healthy to exercise for hours, every single day. Later in the chapter we'll discuss how much exercise is healthy.

6. **True.** Medical studies show that exercise can improve your mood. In fact, when people are mildly or moderately depressed, regular exercise can actually improve their mood as much as medication (if you're very depressed or think about dying, you *must* see a doctor right away). Exercise also gives you energy, so even if you have to force yourself at first, once you get going, your energy level will increase and you won't find it as hard to get motivated the next time.

7. **False.** When specific muscles get a good workout, they may ache afterwards. For example, stair climbing might make your thighs ache and arm raises could make your shoulders or upper arms ache. You might not feel it every time (or ever) and if you don't ache it doesn't mean you didn't have a good workout. The achiness will probably start 24 to 48 hours after you exercise and could last for a few days. Bonnie Goldstein (an awesome athlete who works with teenage girls—who will teach us a lot more later in the chapter) calls it the "muscle flu" and says it is not a reason to stop exercising. In fact, gentle stretching and light exercise can

help you feel better. If you're really hurting, rest that part of your body until it's better and then try again. When you resume exercising, it may help to work out with a little less intensity so you can test your muscles to see how they're feeling. BUT, if you feel sharp pain during or after exercise, make sure you don't exercise again until you've checked with your parent and doctor because if you pull a muscle or otherwise injure yourself, exercise will make it worse.

8. False. Many girls find formal exercise boring or difficult so they won't do it. They also think that if they're enjoying themselves while doing a physical activity (like skating, walking the dog or dancing) it means it's not really exercise. This is not true. As you read on, you'll see that the best way to stick to exercising is to have fun while doing it.

9. True. You may know that exercise is good for your heart and muscles and that it helps give you a healthy feeling and healthy looking body. But just as importantly, moving your body also helps develop strong, healthy bones.

10. False. Some people believe exercise suppresses your appetite. Actually, if you have a good workout you may feel hungry afterwards because your body has depleted its energy supply. So, if you are hungry, it is important to eat healthy food after you work out.

11. False. First, you lose weight by *using up more calories than you take in*. Calories are used up by movement—the greater the movement, the more calories are burned for energy. Calories are taken in by eating food. So if the number of calories you take in by eating is greater than the number of calories used up by exercising, you won't lose weight—no matter how much you exercise. This is why you have to eat healthily and exercise in order to have a healthy body. Second, muscle is *heavier* than fat. As your body becomes stronger through regular exercise, you will develop healthy muscle that will replace areas of your body that contained fat. Since this

muscle is heavier than the fat, your actual weight may not go down (and could even go up). BUT, since *muscle takes up less space than fat, your body will be leaner.*

12. True. Exercise uses calories, gives you energy, improves your mood, and builds muscle, all helping you have the ability, willpower, and energy to lose weight. You then need to maintain a weight that is healthy for your age, height, and frame.

13. False. Sometimes sports or dance can take a large time commitment, but this isn't necessary in order to have a good workout or a healthier lifestyle. As you read on you'll see that there are many ways to fit exercise into your life that take only a little extra time, but still benefit you greatly.

14. False. Exercising has little to do with whether you are thin and lots to do with being healthy. No matter what you look like, you need to exercise in order to make the most of your body, strengthen your heart, and be energetic.

15. False. If you rely only on "watching what you eat" or dieting to change your body, you will struggle to succeed. As we've discussed, it's impossible to constantly deny and restrict yourself. But if you exercise regularly, you won't have to diet. As long as you eat healthily most of the time, your body will use the food you eat to fuel the exercise and you will, over time, become healthier (and lose weight).

16. False. Although it is *very* important to eat enough when you exercise, working out does not make it okay to eat tons of junk food, fast food, or other things that aren't healthy. Having a healthy and nutritious snack or meal is important before and after you exercise, and sometimes eating junk food is fine. But don't use exercise as an excuse to pig out constantly, you'll just get in the way of your own goals of a healthier lifestyle.

So how did you do? If you got thirteen or more correct answers, you're exercise excellent; if you got ten or more, you're almost there;

seven or more and you need to review the facts; and less than seven . . . I'm sure if you've read the correct responses, you'll do better next time! But no matter how you scored, by the time you've finished reading this chapter, you'll be at the top of the class when it comes to exercise knowledge. You will also learn that exercise doesn't have to be intimidating. It can be manageable, fun, and something you won't want to avoid or quit.

As you can see from the quiz, there are many different ways exercise can improve your life, from physically (you'll be more fit), to emotionally (your mood will be better and you'll have more self confidence), to socially (you'll have activities to do with friends). However, the reason you're reading this book is because you want a healthier looking and feeling body. So, if you've decided to *take control of your health,* exercise will play an essential role in your success because:

1. Some of the energy your body needs to exercise will come from the fat cells you're trying to reduce. This will help you stop gaining weight, or if necessary it will help you to lose weight effectively. But too much exercise will overwork and harm your body. With the help of experts, I'll teach you how to find a happy medium.

2. Exercise makes your heart stronger, which gives you the energy to do more in every aspect of your life including improving your ability to exercise and become healthier.

3. Exercise helps you develop strong muscles and—get this—muscle actually requires energy to keep it going (fat just sits there like a blob). So if you exercise steadily and develop more muscle and less fat on your body, you'll actually need to eat more because your body will require energy from food to support your muscle growth. And don't worry about looking like a man! Girls and women don't have the same hormones in their bodies as boys and men. This means they can't develop man-type muscles, except under very rare circumstances like intensive, professional-level weight training.

The First Moves

Before we focus on an exercise program, let's start with a few simple tips that will make movement a part of your everyday life. You can begin to incorporate these into your life immediately, one or two at a time. Add another every few days for two or three weeks before you begin following the ideas in the rest of the chapter.

Tip #1: Music is a must! Get in the habit of taking a personal tape or CD player with headphones everywhere you can. Pick upbeat tunes that make you want to move. All movement helps, even if you're just bopping to the beat a bit. Fast, fun music will make you move a bit faster—you'll be exercising without even realizing it!

Tip #2: Walk as often as possible. Choose the stairs instead of the elevator; walk up the escalator instead of standing; hide the TV remote so you have to get up to change the channel; tell your mom she doesn't have to find the closest parking spot at the mall, then walk swiftly to the store; walk home from school instead of catching a ride.

Tip #3: Sneak some motion into your life while doing other things. Here are some examples:

* While brushing your teeth, rise up and down on the balls of your feet.

* While waiting in line, move your feet side to side, or squeeze and release the muscles in different parts of your body.

* Make homework breaks a time to stretch and walk around for a few minutes.

* When you're talking on the phone, stand or walk around. A cordless phone (or one with a very long cord) is great for this.

- Fidget! Did you know that people who fidget are less likely to be overweight than those who don't—a scientific study proved this.

- While watching TV, stretch or exercise. Don't eat!!

- Use time in the pool to actually swim or walk around in the water. If you don't want to swim then do a few laps around the outside of the pool (on dry land).

- When you're shopping at the mall, walk quickly from store to store. Although it's okay to stop if you see a great outfit!

- Choose social activities that involve movement—later I'll give you lots of ideas.

- Don't get drive-through food. Ask your parent or friend to pull in so you can walk inside to get your food.

- When you go to a school dance, don't just check out the guys—dance!

- Rearrange your room—moving furniture is great exercise and you'll have a fresh new look.

When you start following the suggestions in the rest of the chapter, don't forget about these three tips. The movement you've added to your daily life will help keep your body feeling and looking healthy—no matter what other exercise you add.

Meet Bonnie and Bev

Now you're ready to begin an organized exercise routine. I promised you that this will be manageable and not intimidating—and I will keep my promise. I consulted with two really awesome women, Bonnie Goldstein and Bev Francis, who are both superexperts, not only about exercise, but also about exercise and teenage girls (you can read about them at the end of the book).

Bonnie says you should start with a decent pair of well-fitting sneakers:

- They shouldn't be too tattered—if they look too worn, they are too worn
- They DON'T have to cost a lot of money
- Comfort is key—they should be wide enough and long enough for your foot (this isn't the time to try and squeeze into a smaller size)
- They should be sturdy—not a casual, fashion sneaker
- Brand is NOT important

Additionally, dress in comfortable, lightweight clothes and a well-fitting, supportive bra. If you want to wear official "work-out clothes," that's fine too. There's no right way to dress to exercise as long as you feel comfortable.

Getting Your Doctor's Permission

There is no reason that *most* girls shouldn't exercise. In fact, it is often exactly what the doctor recommends. However, some girls could have medical reasons that may make it difficult for them to do all or some types of exercise. So, before you begin this, or any other exercise program, it is *very important* to make sure it's healthy for your particular body. Show this chapter to your parent and/or doctor and get his or her approval. This is especially true if you know you have a medical concern that could be affected by exercise like asthma, a heart condition or problems with your muscles, bones or joints.

The Part about Privacy

We know that when you're overweight or out of shape it may be embarrassing to exercise in front of people. That's why so many overweight kids and teens hate gym class so much. For this reason, the exercise plan you're about to learn can be done in *total privacy*. Also, it doesn't require very much space so you can do it in your bedroom. Of course, for some girls, exercising with a friend is fun, and this or any other exercise can be done in pairs or groups. Later in the chapter, we'll discuss great ways to pair exercise with socializing. Now, with all the details out of the way, we're ready to begin!

The Timetable

It will take a minimum of six weeks to master the moves. If you already exercise at least once in a while, then six weeks may be an accurate guideline for getting fully into the program. However, if this is the first time you've ever really exercised you shouldn't be discouraged if it takes even longer, because your body may need more time to get used to moving. As you go along, focus on how you're feeling. As long as you keep progressing, it doesn't matter how slowly it goes. Even if you add only five seconds a day to your workout, you've accomplished more than the time before and you should be proud of yourself.

Pay attention to your body at all times. If your heart is pounding out of your chest, slow down. If your legs are feeling sore on a day that you're supposed to work out, it's okay to give them a break and just exercise your upper body. The most important thing is to keep going at a comfortable pace. You deserve a healthy feeling and looking body, so don't give up on yourself.

Weeks One and Two: Start with Stretching

Exercising means you will be moving many different muscles. As you begin to move these muscles, it's important to stretch them too. This is the best way to avoid injuring yourself and it also prepares your body to be able to achieve to its fullest. So, in weeks one and two of the exercise program we focus only on stretching. You will find that while stretching is important, it is quite simple, and doesn't require much time. You can stretch anywhere—inside, outside, watching TV, during a homework break—and it shouldn't take more than five or ten minutes. During weeks one and two you should stretch every other day. After the first two weeks, you should stretch each time before you exercise and again when you're finished (at the end of exercising you don't need to include #1 from the list below (walking), because you're already warmed up.

Okay, here's the stretching routine. The moves are in a logical order, so do one through seven as they are listed. After you've done the whole things a few times, you'll probably have it memorized. If you rush your stretching you'll increase your chances of injury. So count slowly as you hold a stretch, take deep breaths and have fun. Successful stretching strategies are:

1. Walk first: Walk around or in place for three minutes, gently swinging your arms, in order to begin warming up your muscles.

2. Ankles: Sit down on the floor with your legs stretched out in front of you (they can be slightly bent). Rest your palms on the floor behind you and lean back on them slightly. Lift one leg off the floor a little and slowly rotate your ankle five times in one direction and then five times in the other direction. Put your foot down and do the same with the other foot.

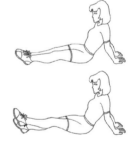

3. Back of leg: Still resting back on your hands, with your legs stretched out in front of you, point your toes up to the ceiling and flex your feet back slightly towards your chest. Hold for a count of five (one Mississippi, two Mississippi, three Mississippi . . .). You should feel a slight pulling (not pain) in your calf muscles (the back of your leg between your knee and ankle). You may also feel it in your *hamstring* muscles (the back of your leg between your knee and rear end). Repeat this movement five times.

4. Back of leg and lower back: With your legs still out in front of you, sit up with your back straight, off your hands. Stretch your arms out in front of you and reach forward as if to grab something just above your toes. Your goal is not to try and reach for your toes. Rather, you are stretching your lower  back muscles. It is fine to bend your knees a bit to do this stretch. Hold the stretching position for as long as possible up to about twenty seconds (twenty Mississippis). If you can only hold it for one or two seconds try to add one second each time you stretch.

5. Back, arms, chest, and stomach: Lie down on your back with your arms straight out above your head and your legs out in front of you straight or slightly bent. Stretch your arms above your head as far as you can, hold for two Mississippis and relax. Repeat this five times.

6. Back: Roll over onto your hands and knees, then without moving your hands or knees, sit back trying to touch your rear end (or glutes) to your heels. You should feel a slight pull in your lower and upper back. Hold this position for as long as possible up to ten Mississippis. Take a deep breath with every couple of counts.

7. Arms, shoulders, and waist: Stand up and stretch your arms above your head reaching toward the ceiling with your fingertips. Hold this for five Mississippis. In this position, clasp your hands together, palms to the ceiling, and with your arms still straight up, lean slowly to one side. If you're leaning to the right, you should feel a slight tug in  your left side, if you're leaning left you should feel the pull in your right side. Be careful not to lean too far to the side, especially the first few times. Hold this position for as long as possible up to five Mississippis. Next, repeat, stretching to the other side in the same way. Release your arms and take a couple of deep breaths.

In these seven simple steps, you can stretch your whole body. However, Bonnie said that even though these stretches are simple, it doesn't mean they will be easy to accomplish right away. She explained that some girls find moving their muscles a bit painful and difficult at first. She also said that if you are very overweight, you might find stretching difficult until you start to reduce some of the excess fat. But don't give up because Bonnie told me something so important that I think you should write it in big letters and stick it up so you can see it every day:

If you can't do it today,
You will be able to do it tomorrow.

Muscle Flu Versus Injury

As you'll remember (quiz answer #7), a day or two after exercising your muscles may ache. Bonnie calls this "muscle flu." Stretching, especially if you're new to it, can cause this too so don't worry and don't stop stretching. Just stretch lightly until you feel better. This will keep you moving forward and it will help your muscles get better. If you have enormous muscle aches it probably means you did too much all at once, so take it a bit easier from now on and take an extra day off if you need to.

But if you feel a sharp pain as you're stretching or right afterwards, you may have pulled a muscle or otherwise injured yourself. Don't keep this to yourself. Tell an adult and see a doctor, if necessary. But don't be discouraged and most of all DON'T QUIT!!! Even the best athletes in the world injure themselves. You'll heal and be ready to go again. If you need to give a muscle time to heal, follow all medical advice (including resting and applying ice or heat). In the mean time, try to keep exercising your other body parts as much as possible.

The Elements of Exercise

After you've practiced stretching for two weeks, the next four weeks will be spent gradually learning how to exercise all the different parts of your body by combining fourteen very simple moves, a few at a time. When Bonnie and Bev created this routine, they kept in mind that teenage girls have busy lives with little time to exercise. I told them I'd promised you a plan that would give you the best chance for success and they promised me that as long as you follow the week by week steps, you *will* be successful.

First, I will describe all fourteen exercises. Bonnie and Bev designed the order of the exercises so they build on each other a little at a time. You will learn to combine the different exercises, and then gradually increase the amount of time you spend exercising. Then you will learn to maintain that level. The fourteen exercises are as follows:

1. Head Turns (loosen the joints in your neck): Stand straight with your arms down at your sides and your legs slightly apart. Look straight ahead of you. Drop your head forward, then slowly raise it and lift it backwards so you're looking at  the ceiling. Bring your head up to face front again. Now, turn your head to the right, back to the middle and then to the left and back to the middle. These five movements, performed in sequence one after the other, make up one head turn.

2. Shoulder Shrugs (strengthen neck muscles): Stand straight, arms down at sides, legs slightly apart. Lift your shoulders to your ears, hold for a second, then drop them again. Repeat this three times then pause for a second before performing the next three shrugs. Three shrugs is one set.

3. Front/Back Shoulder Rolls (strengthen neck and upper back muscles): Stand straight, arms down at sides. Pull your shoulders forward, then lift them up, then roll them backwards while squeezing your shoulder blades (the bones that stick out in your upper back) towards each other and holding the 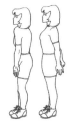 squeeze for as long as possible, up to five seconds. Then bring your shoulders down and repeat this sequence twice more. Next, reverse the direction of your roll, going back with a shoulder blade squeeze, up, forward, and down, repeating this sequence twice more. Three forward and three back rolls is one set.

4. Front Arm Raises (strengthens shoulders): Stand straight, arms resting lightly on the front of your thighs, palms in. Lift your arms straight in front of you (palms still down) to shoulder height (slightly below eye level) and then lower back down. These  two movements count as one arm raise. Each movement should take one Mississippi (one Mississippi up, one Mississippi down; two Mississippis up, two Mississippis down . . .).

5. Side Arm Raises (strengthens shoulders): Stand straight, arms resting lightly on the sides of your thighs, palms in. Lift your arms up to the sides (palms still down) to shoulder height and then lower back down. These two movements counts as one arm raise (same as number 4).

6. Bicep Curls (strengthens bicep muscles— the inner part of your upper arm): Stand straight, arms at your sides, palms and arms facing out in FRONT of you. In this position, make your hands into fists and clench tightly. Now, with your arms still facing front and your fists clenched, bend your arms at

217

your elbows, bringing your fists up toward your shoulders, without moving your upper arms. As your fist reaches the top position, squeeze your upper arms for a second, then release and move your arms back down. This is one curl. Keep your hands as fists until you've finished as many curls as you want to do.

7. Tricep Pushdowns (strengthens tricep muscles— the outer and back part of your upper arm): Stand straight, arms at your sides, wrists bent up, palms facing the floor and fingers pointing forward. Keeping your wrists bent and palms facing down, bend your arms at the elbows until your knuckles or fingers come up to your shoulders. Lower back down. This is one curl. Keep your wrists bent until you've finished as many pushdowns as you want to do.

8. Walking, Marching, Jogging (strengthens your heart, tones your legs, increases your overall fitness level): Start by walking or marching in place around the room, taking small steps. As you become more comfortable (over several days or weeks of exercise), begin to raise your knees higher each time you work out. Also, start to swing your arms a little, and then gradually higher to increase your effort. If marching becomes too easy, slowly increase your speed (over any period of time) until you find you are jogging in place or around the room. You can even alternate marching and jogging. As your heart becomes stronger, you will find that you can gradually increase the amount of time you march or jog before needing to rest (start with ten to thirty seconds per day, and work your way up to twenty minutes, which could take days, weeks or even months).

9. Glute squeezes (tones your upper, rear thigh and butt muscles): Stand up straight with your feet together, arms relaxed at your sides. Now squeeze both sides of your rear end together, hold the

squeeze for two Mississippis and release. Repeat as many times as you want.

10. Squats (strengthens and tones your thighs— upper legs): Stand up straight with your legs about hip width apart. Hold your arms out straight in front of you at shoulder height or folded into a "genie" position. Through- out the exercise it is very important to keep  your arms in this position, your back straight, your head up, your eyes looking straight ahead and most importantly, your stomach pulled in. Strong abdominal (stomach) muscles mean a strong lower back too. Now bend your knees as if you are going to sit down, then stand up straight again—that's the squat. Your goal is to get as close to "sitting" as you can, without collapsing. It can help to have a chair or bench behind you. As you feel your rear end touch the seat of the chair, stand up again—don't actually sit down. If you don't have a chair behind you, *never squat past the sitting point.* It's not good for your knees. In other words, your rear end should not move lower than your knees. If you've never squatted before, you may find it dif- ficult at first to get all the way down. But don't worry, squat as far as you can, while still maintaining your posture. Even if you can only do slight knee bends, remember if you can't do it today, you'll do it tomorrow (or next week, or next month, or . . .) You can also do squats against a wall or door—keep your whole back flat against the wall (don't arch your back) and slide down the wall/door into the sit- ting position, and then up again.

11. Side Lunges (strengthens and tones inner and outer legs): Stand straight with your legs a bit more than hip width apart and your feet turned slightly out. As with squats, you need to keep your back and neck straight, head up, and eyes looking straight ahead through-  out the whole exercise. Hold your arms straight out to the sides at shoulder height, for balance. Now, lunge to the right, bending

your right knee, while keeping your left leg straight. Lunge as low as you can without letting your rear end go lower than your knee (if you go too low it will strain your knee). Then come back up to the starting position and, without stopping repeat to the left. One

to each side counts as one lunge. Lunges should be done slowly and carefully for the best results. Repeat as many times as you want. Like squats, lunges can be tough at first. So if you've never done them before, don't try to lunge too deeply, or too many times.

12. Kick-Backs (strengthens and tones the back of your thighs and your rear end): Face a wall or the back of a chair or a table. Rest your hands lightly on the wall, table or chair back for balance, without leaning heavily for support. While standing on your left leg, bend  your right knee up slightly and flex your right ankle so your toes are pointing at the ground. Keep your ankle flexed throughout the exercise. Now, kick your foot back straight as if you're kicking something just behind you. As you straighten your leg behind you, keep your ankle flexed and squeeze your right butt muscle for one-one thousand. Then bring your leg back in again. Repeat this as many times as you want. Then put your right foot down and repeat the exercise with your left leg. Keep your upper body straight and stable throughout the exercise—don't move it around.

13. Wall Push-ups (strengthens and tones arms, shoulders, chest, stomach, back): Stand straight, facing a wall (or closed door) with your arms outstretched, close enough so that your palms are both flat against the wall, slightly more than shoulder width apart. Now, keeping your palms on the wall, take one small step backwards so you have to lean slightly into the wall. You should

maintain this position throughout the exercise. To do the wall push-up, bend your arms so that you are moving your nose as close to the wall as possible without touching it. Then use your arms and chest to push you back up to the starting position. This is one push-up. Repeat as many times as you want. It is VERY important NOT to move your head or neck during the push-up. Your arms and chest should be doing all the work. Also, don't let your back sink down toward the floor. Rather use your stomach and back muscles to keep your back, neck, and legs in one straight line throughout the exercise. Push-ups are just about the most awesome exercise because they work practically your whole body. **If you had to pick just one exercise to do, this would be the one!!** But it has to be done right. So, take the time to practice slowly, checking frequently to make sure that your technique and posture are good. Remember, do the best you can! At first you may be able to do only one or two, and you may not get your nose anywhere near the wall. But don't give up—you'll definitely get there eventually.

14. Bent Knee Push-ups (work all the same body parts as wall push-ups, just better). You may find it difficult to do these until you've lost some weight and gained some strength. But as long as you work on everything you're learning in this book, you will be able to do them eventually. Get down on your hands and knees  with your hands slightly more than shoulder width apart and a bit further front than your nose. Now, shift your weight forwards, onto your hands so that your hips move closer to the ground and your back, butt, and upper legs are in one straight line. Use your stomach muscles to keep you in this position throughout the whole exercise. DON'T let your stomach drop toward the ground.

Next, bend your arms so that your nose comes as close as possible to the ground without you falling. Then use your arms and chest to push you back up again. Your stomach, back, and legs should not be doing the work at all. This is one push-up. Do as many as you want to do. When you've mastered these, all you need to do to convert them into real push-ups is to straighten out your legs and do the push-up from the balls of your feet, rather than from your knees—you go girl!!

Reminders and Thoughts for your New Routine

→ Start small and don't feel pressure to increase the amount of time you exercise until you are ready.

→ Don't worry that these exercises will turn fat into muscle, making you look huge. Muscle and fat can't turn into each other, and remember, girls don't have the hormones to become super muscular. Along with healthy eating, these exercises will help you become healthier, leaner, and stronger.

→ Sometimes, when girls have excess fat on their bodies, they feel uncomfortable moving too much because they don't like the jiggling, bouncing feelings as they move. These fourteen exercises really keep bouncing and jiggling to a minimum. However, in number eight, if you jog instead of marching, you may feel bouncy or uncomfortable. But *you don't have to jog if you don't want to,* just keep marching and swinging your arms for an excellent workout with very few jiggles.

→ Exercising doesn't have to be complicated in order to work. Although these fourteen exercises are very simple they will get the job done.

→ Try to be consistent about when you exercise. Pick a time of day, certain days of the week or while you're watching a particular

TV show to get your exercise done. Think about whether you're a *morning* or *evening* person. For example, if you're an evening person, don't try to wake up early to exercise—it'll never work.

→ If the plan seems too much to begin with, pick just one or two days a week to start exercising. For example, maybe you can manage only weekends. That's fine as long as you gradually but consistently add on (even if it's only a few seconds or minutes and eventually a day at a time).

→ Don't forget your music. It'll really get you going, even when you're tired. Also, it's fine to watch TV while you're working out. In fact for some girls, watching TV makes exercising seem less "scary" or overwhelming.

→ Breathe—throughout all the exercises. There's no special way to do it, just keep breathing as you're moving and never hold your breath.

→ Think about your posture. For example, anytime you're standing or walking, keep your shoulders back and your back straight. You'll strengthen your stomach and back muscles, breathe better, and you'll feel and look strong and proud!

→ Keep your abdominal (stomach) muscles pulled in as much as possible while doing all the stretches and exercises—but don't hold your breath while you're doing so. It could take some practice to learn how to hold in your muscles while still breathing. Don't become discouraged if you can't do it right away.

You may have noticed that we don't talk about working out with exercise weights. This is because there is a great deal of controversy about whether it is healthy for children and teenagers to exercise with anything other than their own body weight. Some experts feel that using barbells, dumbbells, and weight machines can slow down the bone growth of teens. Since this is a potentially serious concern, I strongly suggest that you *not* do any of the fourteen exercises (or any other exercise for that matter) using weights, until you have spoken to your doctor. In addition, you should also speak to an exercise professional who specializes in teens to get the latest information about the safety of teens exercising with weights.

Week Three

Now we're ready to continue. This week make sure you're familiar with exercises one through seven. Before beginning, you will need a watch, clock, or timer. To keep things simple I will always start each week on Monday, but if you'd like to use a different schedule (e.g., start your week on Wednesday) go right ahead. Just keep the exercise days in the same order as mine. Make sure to keep your body straight and don't rush. Also, *don't forget to include stretching each time before and after you work out*. Okay, let's go!

Monday: Three head turns followed by three sets of shoulder shrugs, followed by three sets of the front/back shoulder roll sequence. Repeat this routine (head turns, shoulder shrugs, shoulder rolls) for five minutes (look at the clock or set a timer).

Tuesday: Ten front arm raises, followed by ten side arm raises. Repeat this sequence for five minutes.

Wednesday: Ten bicep curls followed by ten tricep curls. Repeat this sequence for five minutes.

Thursday: Repeat Monday's routine.

Friday: Repeat Tuesday's routine.

Saturday: Repeat Wednesday's routine.

Sunday: Take the day off, but *do something*, like walk the dog, stroll around the block or take a bike ride.

Note: The exercise in week three shouldn't cause muscle achiness, but if it does, just stretch gently and, if necessary, take a day or two off until you feel better.

Week Four

Now, we'll add exercises eight through thirteen, so become familiar with how to do these and have your clock or timer handy. If you need to rest during an exercise before the time is up, go ahead. Then pick it up again, adding together all your time spent moving, until you've completed the specified amount of minutes for that segment (e.g., on Monday you may march for two minutes, rest a minute, and then march for the last three minutes). Continue to focus on doing the exercises carefully, without rushing. Also, remember to stretch before and after each work out.

Monday: March for five minutes

Tuesday: Butt squeezes for one minute, squats for one minute and side lunges for one minute.

Wednesday: Three head turns, followed by three sets of shoulder shrugs, followed by three sets of the front/back shoulder roll sequence. Repeat this routine (head turns, shoulder shrugs, shoulder rolls) for five minutes and then do wall push-ups for five minutes.

Thursday: Ten front arm raises, followed by ten side arm raises. Repeat this sequence for five minutes. Ten bicep curls followed by ten tricep curls. Repeat this sequence for five minutes.

Friday: Ten squats, ten lunges, and ten kick-backs. Then repeat this sequence for five minutes. Next, march for five minutes and finally do wall push-ups for five minutes. If you like, you can do two-and-a-half minutes of push-ups before you march and then the rest afterwards.

Saturday: Off, but take a walk, work in the garden, or clean your room—some kind of movement.

Sunday: Off, same as Saturday.

You increased your movement a bit in week four, so you might find yourself beginning to sweat a bit. These are signs that you're doing the right thing!! Your body is thanking you for it, and I bet you're feeling really proud of yourself. If you're ready to move on to week five's routine go right ahead. But if week four's routine was tough then stick with it for another week or more if necessary until you're feeling that it isn't a struggle.

Week Five

By now you're familiar with the stretching and exercise sequences and you're doing great. So in week five, we'll increase the energy level slightly more. If you find week five really challenging, you should stick with this routine for more than a week (as you may have done for week four) before going on to week six. After a couple of weeks your heart will become stronger, you won't lose your breath so quickly and you won't be as achy. Try and add thirty seconds to a minute every other time you march (or more often if you can do it). Just keep blasting the tunes and moving your body! Remember to keep stretching.

Note: By now your exercise routine should be taking you approximately twenty to thirty minutes to complete each time. I don't want you to give up exercising because you feel that you don't have the time to fit in your busy schedule. So, if you find that you don't have the full time, it is okay to break up your routine. For example, for Monday's routine (below) you may do number's 1, 2, and 3 in the morning, but then save the marching for later in the day when you have more time. Try not to do this every time you exercise, but even if you have to do it every time, it's okay because *any* exercise is better than no exercise.

Monday: (1) Three head turns, followed by three sets of shoulder shrugs, followed by three sets of the front/back shoulder roll sequence. Repeat this routine (head turns, shoulder shrugs, shoulder rolls) for five minutes. (2) Ten front arm raises, followed by ten side arm raises. Repeat this sequence for five minutes. (3) Ten bicep curls followed by ten tricep pushdowns. Repeat this sequence for five minutes. March for five minutes (or more if you can).

Tuesday: Off, but dance in your bedroom, walk home from school, or play Frisbee in the park.

Wednesday: Butt squeezes, squats, and side lunges, each for one and-a-half minutes; wall push-ups for five minutes.

Thursday: March for ten minutes. If you get tired, slow down then start again until you've done a total of ten minutes.

Friday: Off, but catch a ball with a friend, do some laundry or baby-sit a toddler—you know the drill—just keep moving!

Saturday: Same as Monday.

Sunday: Same as Thursday. If you can increase the time or intensity of your marching, go for it.

Week Six

This is the final week of the program, but it's only the beginning of your exercising life. This is the most intense of all the weeks, so keep working at whatever pace is comfortable for you. Don't forget your stretching. Take as many weeks as necessary to feel that you can complete this routine successfully.

Monday: The first thirteen exercises as you have been doing them, adding time and intensity to your marching at a slow and steady pace.

Tuesday: Same as Monday, but substitute bent knee push-ups for the wall push-ups.

Wednesday: Off, but keep moving.

Thursday: Same as Monday.

Friday: Same as Tuesday.

Saturday: Off, but keep moving.

Sunday: March or jog or a march/jog combination for up to twenty minutes.

When you've accomplished week six (which as you know could take more than six weeks) spend the next two months alternating weekly between the week five and week six routines. Continue to add time to your marching until you're up to twenty minutes. There's no specific time for how long it should take for you to get there, just keep working at it. After two months you can increase past twenty minutes or you can increase the intensity of your marching by using your arms, lifting your legs higher, and even jogging. Don't increase your marching/jogging time past thirty minutes. Remember, *too much exercise is as unhealthy as too little.* You should also gradually increase the number of repetitions you do of exercises—particularly squats, lunges, and push-ups. Keep doing them in sets of ten, working your way up to three sets of ten repetitions each. There is no need to do more than this. You can continue alternating between weeks five and six and you can also experiment with doing the exercises in different orders.

Some girls like to keep a log or a journal to chart their progress over weeks or months. If you're the journaling type, you might enjoy keeping track on how much time you spend marching, and how many repetitions you complete of different exercises.

What about Abs?

Abdominal or "ab" muscles as they're often called, are your stomach muscles. Your abs get worked whenever you stand up straight and hold your back and stomach strongly while doing other exercises. But as with any other muscle, it's a good idea to strengthen them specifically. Strong abs can also help prevent back problems. However, like all muscles, abs should not be exercised every day, and millions of sit-ups or crunches won't give you that sleek, bikini belly you may wish for. In fact, you may have fabulous abdominal muscles, but if they're covered with a layer of fat, you'll never see them. For your stomach to look flatter, you need to have less fat on and around it, which you will get from exercising and eating healthily, whether or not you specifically target your abdominal muscles. Bottom line: Working out your abdominals is not crucial to your physical health, so if you don't feel like doing them for the first few weeks (or ever) it's fine.

To give your abdominals a fair work out, Bonnie and Bev suggest exercising them twice a week. Pick whichever two days you like and add them to your routine. Don't do two days in a row though, because the break will give the muscles a chance to rest between workouts. Your abdominal routine is as follows:

Sit-ups (strengthens your stomach muscles):  Lie on your back with your knees bent and your feet hooked under a bed, chair, or couch. Alternatively, you could ask someone to hold your ankles lightly. Place your arms on the floor at your sides with your palms facing the floor. Lift your upper body about six inches off the ground, straight up toward the ceiling (not toward your feet) then release back down. This is one sit-up. During these movements, keep your chin tucked into your chest and your belly button pushed in, curving your upper body inwards toward your lower back. Use your hands for support on the floor, if you need to, but don't use your head and neck to pull you up. These should be kept in a straight line with your spine. Your stomach muscles do the work. Repeat up to ten times, resting if you need to. If you can't do ten, build up slowly over days or weeks. After these become easier, you can increase to up to thirty and you can also try them with your hands behind your head (elbows pointing sideways) or folded over your chest. You can also do partner sit-ups: Instead of a bed or chair, you and a friend sit facing each other, lock ankles, and do the sit-ups in unison.

Knee lifts (strengthens lower stomach muscles): Lie on your back, arms at your sides close to your hips, with your knees bent on the floor. Slowly lift your feet, bringing your knees in to your chest then lower back down so your toes just touch the floor. Repeat or work up to ten times. After you have mastered this you can increase to up to thirty repetitions.

Sit-ups with resistance (strengthens front and side stomach muscles): You will need a full two-liter soda bottle for this exercise (a used bottle, filled with water is fine). Lie on your back, feet on the floor, knees bent. Hold the

bottle lengthways between your hands (one hand grabbing the cap side and the other holding the bottom of the bottle) with your arms stretched out above your head. Moving the bottle forward, with your arms still straight, lift your body slightly, until you feel your stomach muscles tightening a bit. Next, rock the bottle very slightly up and down and then slightly to the left and right. Do as many as you can, up to ten. If it's hard to do even one, work on the sit-ups without rocking for a while, then gradually add in the rocking. When you've mastered this, you can increase up to thirty repetitions.

What's Next?

Once you've been doing the full routine (with or without abdominals) for three months, you may want to consider going to a gym to try some classes, or some treadmill or stair climbing machines. Make sure you consult with one of the fitness professionals before using any of the equipment, so you don't injure yourself. You may also want to explore some exercise videos. There are many different kinds of wonderful exercise techniques other than the ones in this book (like yoga, martial arts, pilates, kickboxing, aerobics, and step). The best way to see which ones best fit your personality is to try them out. You can take videos out of the library for free, rather than buying them. This way you can also exchange them whenever you get bored. Start with beginner videos and then, as you need more of a challenge, progress to more advanced versions.

If you want to continue exercising privately, you can read fitness magazines and books to get ideas for variations on how to work the different muscle groups and to find alternatives to marching and jogging in place. Try everything slowly and carefully. Many fitness magazines contain exercises that don't require fancy equipment or weights. If you find exercises you like, cut them out and try them. Look for exercises that work all the different body parts that we've discussed. If you're not sure whether you're doing it right, speak to a fitness professional, or skip that exercise.

The Water Watch

As you continue exercising, you will eventually sweat. Sweat may seem disgusting or feel uncomfortable, but it means your body is working. However, when you sweat, and even when you don't, your body loses water. In fact the human body is made up of 65 percent water and every day we lose some through our skin, as well as through urinating, sweating, and crying. Your body needs water to survive. When you exercise, you lose water at a much higher rate than when you don't. This is true even if you don't realize you're sweating. So, you must make up for the water loss. Bonnie came up with a very simple plan to make sure you get enough water.

The water plan follows along with your exercise plan:

→ Starting in week one drink one glass (8 ounces, a ½ pint water bottle) of water each time before you exercise.

→ During week two *add* a glass of water after you finish exercising (drink slowly).

→ In week three *add* a glass of water when you wake up or brush your teeth.

→ At the start of week four *add* a glass of water each day at lunch.

→ Start week five by *adding* a glass of water with each afternoon snack.

→ In week six *add* a glass of water each night at dinner.

→ Start week seven by *adding* a glass of water with an evening snack or before bed. If drinking late at night wakes you up to go to the bathroom, adjust your schedule until you can fit all eight glasses in earlier in the day.

If eight glasses of water makes you feel flooded or spend all day in the bathroom, adjust down to six or seven, but don't go much below six glasses of water a day. Also, sip water during exercise, but don't drink too much right before or during a workout because you might get stomach cramps. Remember, water is better for you than any other fluid, but if you just can't stand it, substitute flavored seltzer or fruit flavored water. Don't substitute juice, tea, soda, or coffee for water.

Terrific Teen Tip: Chantal, an athletic teen and one of the girls in my Advisory Group, had some excellent advice. She said, "Girls shouldn't think that they have to do boring exercises to stay in shape. They can do things they enjoy like dancing or acting." To prove this is true, Jaime and Montserrat, two other girls in the group made a list of thirty really fun activities that don't seem like exercise, but, guess what, they are! How many do you do?

Jaime's Jams and Monsie's Moves

1. Bike ride to a friend's house

2. Rollerblade or rollerskate (wear protective gear!)

3. Downhill or cross-country ski

4. Take a kickboxing class—imagine the punching bag is your worst teacher

5. Swim or dive (can you do the high dive?)

6. Baseball or softball at the park

7. Shoot hoops in the driveway

8. Yoga—take a class or get a video—good exercise and a great destressor

9. Walk with a friend—anywhere and everywhere

10. Jump rope—when was the last time you played double dutch?

11. Dance 'til you drop

12. Ice-skate

13. Tennis—with a friend or alone against a wall

14. Walk the dog

15. Skateboard or try a scooter (wear protective gear!)

16. Play Frisbee

17. Try a karate class—it's very empowering

18. Take a tap or jazz class

19. Try a pottery class—an excellent workout for your hands, arms, and back

20. Go to the playground and swing and climb the monkey bars (just don't scare the little kids)

21. Get a job that involves more than just sitting in one place (you'll make some money too!)

22. Try out the treadmills and step machines in the sports store (maybe you'll meet a cute sales guy too)

23. Go to the zoo or aquarium—it's really fun and you'll walk a lot

24. Go to an amusement park—you'll be running from ride to ride and I think screaming on the roller coaster is also exercise

25. Do some gardening—some girls tell me this is their favorite activity ever

26. Try on all your clothes to see what you still like

27. Take a first aid class—you'll learn how to save someone's life and get exercise too

28. Learn a new sport—any sport at all

29. Babysit—and really play with the kids

30. Clean the car—the water and suds are really fun on a hot day and your mom or dad will be thrilled

Wow, you've really accomplished a lot. Now, the key is to keep going and not lose interest, right? In the next chapter, I'm going to help you stay focused, keep on feeling good, and reaching your goals.

Motivation Is A Must

The Barrier to a Healthier You

People don't often think about motivation as an important part of a healthy life. However, after meeting many times with the girls in my Advisory Group, I discovered that for many girls, staying motivated is the most difficult part about trying to become healthier. Jaime explains how lack of motivation has affected her:

> **"**I'll start out doing great. But then after a few days it gets hard to stay motivated and I'll stop exercising or I'll start eating the wrong things.
>
> Actually, I've heard similar stories from many different girls. They start out with good intentions—eating healthily and exercising daily. But then after a few days, a few weeks or a few months they just can't keep it up.**"**

Like Jaime, Amanda (age 16) has struggled with her weight for about eight years. *"It's the most frustrating thing in the world! I've lost*

and gained the same thirty pounds three times because I can't stay moti-
vated enough to stick to a diet. Now I'm about ready to give up even trying
to diet. I might just accept that I'm always going to be thirty pounds over-
weight" Why is it that girls like Jaime, Amanda, and so many others
have awesome intentions, but then find it difficult or impossible to stay
motivated?

Actually there is more than one answer to this question. For some
girls, difficulty remaining motivated has to do with how they set up
their goals in the first place. For others, it has to do with fears about
change—even if the change is for the better. It could even be about
both these things. We'll look at the top ten barriers to becoming
healthier and you will learn ways to bust the barriers so you *can* stay
motivated. Real success, for the rest of your life, is just a chapter away,
so read on.

Motivation Barrier # 1: Setting Unreachable Weight Loss or Clothes Size Goals

Picture this: You're finally psyched to get healthy. You're ready to exercise and to lose weight. This is a good thing. You've read somewhere that
it's good to lose up to two pounds a week. So you do some quick calcu-
lating and tell yourself that at the end of three months you will have lost
twenty-four pounds. This is a bad thing because setting up such struc-
tured goals for weight loss is almost guaranteed to end in failure.

No matter what you've read, there is absolutely no basis for the idea
that you should lose a certain number of pounds a week. In the first
week or two of eating healthily and exercising, you are likely to drop
a few pounds quite quickly. But this is almost entirely water that your
body is getting rid of, not actual fat. After that, you may lose a half
a pound to a pound each week, but if you're losing more than this it

probably means you're restricting your food intake too much or exercising too often. This isn't healthy for your body and it is very hard to keep it up over the long haul. It's even possible that you will go weeks without losing any weight—this is normal. If you expect to lose more weight than is realistic, you're sure to lose your motivation when this doesn't happen.

What about clothing sizes? Sometimes girls wish they could be a certain clothing size (usually much smaller than their current size) and then they make this size their goal. Unfortunately, this is almost always a recipe for failure because weight loss is only one of the things that will affect your clothing size. As we've discussed, genetics and your body shape also have a huge impact on what size clothing you should wear when you are at a healthy weight. Furthermore, since different clothing companies fit you differently, you may be one size in one brand or style and another size in a second brand or style.

Breaking the Barrier

Don't set large goals for how much weight you think you should lose or what size you believe you should wear. And don't set any time frame for how long it should take you to feel healthy. Instead, focus on how you feel about your body. As you become healthier, you will start to feel more self-confident, happy, and comfortable in your body. Your body image will improve and you will no longer see yourself as "fat," "overweight," or "different" from other girls. Numbers are meaningless, the real deal is in how happy, self-confident, and healthy you feel. If it is difficult for you to ignore the scale all together, set very small goals and don't put any time limit on how long it will take you to reach them. For example, focus on losing a pound or two. Stick with *Dr. Susan's Girls-Only Weight Loss Guide* and don't weigh yourself more than once a week. Once you have reached your first small goal, set another one for yourself to reach. Remember to *always* check that your health specialist doesn't think you're losing too much weight or losing it too quickly.

Motivation Barrier # 2: Restricting Your Eating Too Much or Dieting

For many girls the decision to "lose weight" or become healthy is very difficult. This is because they assume that they will have to give up all the foods they love. They want so much to lose weight that they make up their minds to cut out all the sweets, ice cream, bread, pasta, and pizza. Instead they live on plain tuna, cottage cheese, vegetables, and salad. Some girls even think it's healthy to eat like this so they go on a diet that promotes it. But, as we've discussed, practically all diets fail. Deprivation diets only work while you're on them. Once you "go off" the diet, you go right back to eating the way you were and, like Amanda, you gain back the weight. Dieting and deprivation do not teach you healthy eating or motivate you to have a healthier lifestyle, they just give you a few rules that only work when you're following them exactly. Motivation is really tough if you fail as soon as you stop following the rules! It's also very difficult to stay motivated while you're on a diet, because no one else is doing it. What's more, most diets do not provide adequate nutrients for kids and teens and it's *not* healthy to deprive yourself because your body needs a variety of foods to grow properly.

Next, dieting and deprivation are one of the biggest squelchers of motivation I have ever seen! It is almost impossible to eat in such a restricted way for more than a few days (or a few weeks if you really try). You're bound to slip up eventually and when you do, you'll probably go crazy eating all the foods you've deprived yourself of for so long. Then you lose your motivation completely because you feel like you just don't have what it takes.

Breaking the Barrier

Stay away from diets! By relying on your own brain and decision-making powers to guide and motivate you, you will learn how to make healthy choices for life, rather than for only the time that you're following a diet. The fabulous changes that you feel and see will then continue to motivate you. Stick with *Dr. Susan's Girls-Only Weight Loss Guide* to help you make the best choices for your body. Also, trust yourself to learn how to eat healthily without depriving yourself. Even if it takes longer than you would ideally like, it will ensure that you can stick with it forever. Isn't that what you really want!

Motivation Barrier #3: Overdoing the Exercise

You've heard it a million times: exercise, exercise, exercise! However, when some girls make up their minds to exercise they go from one extreme (not exercising at all) to the other (exercising every day for long periods of time). When you do this, you may start off motivated, but you will soon burn out. Your body will start to hurt, you'll feel exhausted all the time, and you'll begin to dread the workouts. Your good intentions will end in a return to no exercise at all. Is getting healthy supposed to feel this bad?

Breaking the Barrier

Sticking with exercise and doing it consistently is one of the keys to becoming and more importantly to *staying* healthy. But if you overwhelm yourself by taking on too much at once, you'll never be able to stick with it and your motivation will crash. You will be much more likely to stay motivated if you get into exercise gradually. You also need to find activities that fit your life style, and that are simple and fun. Check out Chapter 11 again to learn how to introduce exercise gradually and find exercises that are manageable and fun. Even after you've been exercising for a while, don't make drastic leaps in your exercise routine. For example, don't go from a beginner exercise video to one that is advanced. In between, there is surely an intermediate tape that you can try.

Motivation Barrier #4: Comparing Yourself to Other People

One of the quickest ways to lose your motivation to a healthier life is to start comparing yourself to other people. In every aspect of life there are always going to be people who are thinner, prettier, richer, more popular, more fashionable, taller, shorter, and smarter than you. Some of these people may be in your family and some may be in your school. When you spend your time trying to figure out how you measure up to them it will quickly deflate your motivation to be the best YOU that you can be.

Breaking the Barrier

When you compare yourself unfavorably to someone else it's not because you really want to be that person. Rather, you'd like to be as happy as you think they are because it's likely that you're not feeling very good about yourself or your body. However, as you probably know by now, feeling better about yourself can only be achieved by making the decision to change your body! So, the only comparison you need to make is between the "you" before you decided to become healthier and the "you" after you begin to make those changes. I am confident that when you make this comparison, you will see that the healthier "you" is also happier, more self-confident and more energetic. What's more, although it certainly doesn't feel good to stand out as very overweight, *the way you look is not the only key to all happiness!!!* Achieving a particular size or weight compared to others will not fix all your problems. So, instead, focus on what you *really* want, which is to be happier inside your own body as well as out. Then use this book to make it happen!

Motivation Barrier #5: Focusing Only on the Future

Do you lie in bed at night wondering how popular, pretty, sexy, or happy you'll become once you lose weight or get in shape? I know that I used to do it all the time when I was a teenager. But, I have since discovered, that focusing only on the future can be a real motivation killer. When you focus only on the future you don't notice the small changes that are happening right now. For example, while you're dreaming about running in a 5K race, you might not be patting yourself on the back for having added five minutes to your exercise routine. And if you don't acknowledge the small changes, you'll soon lose your motivation to keep making them.

Breaking the Barrier

When it comes to exercise or eating, it's fine to set reasonable goals for the future, but don't forget to pay attention to how you're doing right now. Recognize that the small steps you're taking all add up to your future and that every single one is important. So each time you make a healthy food choice or exercise a little more strongly you are motivating yourself to keep going.

Terrific Teen Tip: Linda (age 15) keeps a journal of all the positive changes she makes in her life. She writes down healthier eating choices, exercise goals she's reached, and positive changes in how she interacts with her family and friends. She writes the journal like a diary and whenever she's feel a dip in motivation she rereads part or all of it. Linda says that even though it's difficult to see changes on a daily basis, reading her journal reminds her how far she's come.

241

Motivation Barrier # 6: Choosing Immediate Gratification Too Often

When you were very young, do you remember becoming frustrated when your mom or dad would say "No, you can't have another cookie" or "You'll have to wait until later to watch TV"? By saying "No" sometimes, your parents were trying to teach you not to expect to have your desires fulfilled (gratified) immediately. Learning to cope with not getting our desires gratified right away is a very important life lesson. We need it everywhere—waiting in line, sitting in traffic, taking turns, and not getting everything we want. It is also very important for learning how to say NO to more food or NO to going shopping rather than exercising. Some girls have a very hard time not gratifying their own immediate desires. If this sounds like you (you don't say NO to yourself very often), it can be difficult to stay motivated to become healthier. For example, if you're faced with an ice-cream sundae, you'll have a difficult time becoming healthier or losing weight because you will want to allow yourself to eat that sundae. But, if you're able to sometimes say NO to the sundae and put off your desire for immediate gratification in exchange for something more important—your health—you'll find it much easier to stay motivated.

Wanting immediate gratification can also crash your motivation if you don't see results immediately. It can take a month or more to start to see real results from a healthier lifestyle. But if you expect the changes to happen right away you may lose your motivation to continue.

Breaking the Barrier

It is possible to learn how to resist giving in to immediate gratification by visualizing your goals. Tell yourself that by saying "no" to this ice-cream sundae, extra slice of pizza, or chance to skip exercising, you are trading in immediate gratification for a *huge* payoff in the future—looking and feeling much better. Of course, you shouldn't say "no" to everything. Rather, as you know from Chapters 7, 8, and 9, it's all about moderation and portion control. You may say "no" to the sundae, but have a scoop of frozen yogurt instead. You may not skip exercising, but you may have a shorter workout so there's still time to go shopping with your friends (hey, walking energetically around the mall and trying on clothes could even be exercise—you can tell your parents I said that!). By making these choices you will also teach yourself that good things really do come to those who wait!

Motivation Barrier # 7: Fearing Change

Rate the following statements as (1) never/not at all, (2) sometimes, (3) often/always:

_____ 1. I like to change around the furniture in my room to get a different look.

_____ 2. I enjoy shocking myself and others with a totally radical haircut.

_____ 3. I really like to try new foods and different restaurants.

_____ 4. I prefer breaking up to staying with a guy I don't adore.

_____ 5. I love the change in routine that comes with a new school year.

_____ 6. I like traveling to somewhere I've never been rather than going back to the same place again.

_____ 7. I don't mind trying out a new activity, even if no one else I know will be there.

_____ 8. I shop at a variety of stores, rather than always shopping at the same one or two places that I know I like.

Scoring: Count the number of 1s, 2s and 3s.

	Score		Score		Score
1.		2.		3.	

Scoring

If you got mostly "3s," you're the Champion of Change. In fact, you live for it. For you, fearing the change to healthier eating is not your personal barrier. You'll jump right in, try it out and give it your all. A word of caution: you'll have to be careful that you don't change right back to your unhealthy ways if things get a bit boring. Be careful not to change so much that you can't maintain it. Don't sabotage yourself. Make slow changes and learn to stick with them for the long haul.

If you got mostly "2s," consider yourself the Mistress of Moderation. You will make the changes slowly and carefully, but with conviction. You are likely to have great success at becoming healthier because slow change is the most likely to be successful and long term.

If you got mostly "1s," you are the Sweetheart of Sameness. When people don't like to make any changes—even those that are good for them—it is usually because they are in some way afraid of the change. But being fearful of change can be a real barrier to become healthier. Many girls start off motivated, but when their fears kick in they seem to suddenly lose their motivation to be healthier.

Breaking the Barrier

Ask yourself, "What am I afraid of?" For some girls the answer will be that they are afraid of failing—so if you don't try, you can't fail. But trust me when I say failure is not something to be feared. We all fail in different ways, at different times in our life. In fact, we learn more from our failures (because they make us think) than we learn from our successes. Furthermore, there is really no way to fail at becoming healthier. Even if you make only one tiny change you are already successful. What's more, if you follow the other barrier breakers by not trying to do too much at once, you won't set yourself up for losing your motivation to better health.

Other girls are actually afraid of success. Sometimes giving up a way of life or even letting go of the fat on your body can feel like a loss. After all, it's been a part of your identity, your sense of self and your body image for a very long time. Perhaps, too, your larger size has enabled you to avoid the pressures of dating and intimacy. Or maybe unhappiness with your body has masked other serious sadness in your life (divorce, death, school or friendship problems) that you've been able to keep hidden because everyone thinks your unhappiness is about your weight. By giving up your larger size, you expose yourself to becoming vulnerable in all these other ways. If these feelings make sense to you, it's important to share them with an adult you trust. Don't be afraid to ask for help in understanding and managing your feelings. This way, fears or sadness won't get in the way of you feeling happier about your body. You will only be able to break the "fear of change" barrier when you acknowledge your fears and work hard to fight them.

Some girls pretend to themselves and others that they are not unhappy with their bodies, when deep inside they really are. They are afraid that making a lifestyle change may mean acknowledging the truth about how they feel, not only to themselves but to others as well. Admitting this can make some girls feel very vulnerable and can become an enormous barrier.

Speaking about your feelings to people you trust, and writing about your feelings in a journal, can help you to become comfortable revealing the real you. It's okay to be vulnerable and to admit that you'd like to change some aspects of your life. The only way to find the true you is to peel away the layers that have been protecting your wonderful inner self from being revealed.

Motivation Barrier #8:
Not Telling Your Friends

Some girls are able to make healthy changes and lose weight without enlisting the help of anyone at all. But for many girls, the support and encouragement they receive from friends can be a huge motivator. If your friends don't realize that you're trying hard to make changes, they may, without realizing it, encourage you to eat more foods than you need ("c'mon, just one more slice of pizza"), or discourage you from exercising ("it's okay to skip it, let's go to shopping instead"). It can be tough to stay motivated when you're being pressured rather than supported.

Breaking the Barrier

You can enlist the help of your friends by explaining to them how you are beginning to live a healthier life style. Many girls are thrilled that, when given the chance, their friends are very supportive and helpful. If your friends are an important part of your life and really care about you, their interest in helping you become healthier can really motivate you.

Many girls also find it very motivating to work out with a friend or in groups. They encourage each other to push a little further and they support each other when the going gets tough. You may not feel like doing this right away, but once you're feeling a bit more comfortable with your body and energy level, you may want to try exercising with a friend or two.

Terrific Teen Tip: Ashley (age 16) had been dieting on and off for two years, to try and fit in with the other girls in her group. She eventually decided to enlist their help: "I told my friends that I wanted to lose some weight and learn how to exercise better. Before I knew it, they were giving me awesome tips for healthy eating (finally I could stop dieting!), and we all started walking around the school track together after school three days a week. It was great to have their support. Now I don't feel like the odd one out, and we're all getting in better shape!"

Motivation Buster #9: Doing It for All the Wrong Reasons

One of the biggest barriers to motivation is trying to lose weight or change your life style in order to stop your mother's nagging, to attract a guy or to impress your friends. It's not bad if these are part of what motivates you to start thinking about becoming healthier. But doing it for a guy, or any other reason will not be enough to help you keep yourself feeling good for the rest of your life. What happens if the guy isn't interested in you or your mom stops nagging or you have a fight with your friends? The truth is, that it's impossible to stay motivated unless you truly feel that not only do you want to change your body, but that you're ready to make the life changes and do the emotional work necessary to feel better about yourself. You have to do it because you want to look and feel better for yourself, not for anyone else.

Breaking the Barrier

After you've read this book, write a list of all the reasons for which you want to change your lifestyle. Include the reasons that you'd like to lose weight. Be honest with yourself. If your list seems to be about pleasing other people, rather than becoming healthier and happier, it's probably not yet the right time for you to begin. If your list is mixed—some reasons are about wanting to be happier and healthier but others are about getting your parents off your back or impressing your friends or a guy, focus on the first set of reasons. Remember, only you live inside your body, and only you really need to feel good about yourself. It would be nice if your parents were happy, or if other kids were impressed, but these things are not essential in order for you to feel happy with yourself.

When you realize that losing weight and becoming healthier are a gift you can give yourself, you will become motivated to make the choices and changes you want to make. You will soon begin to look and feel healthier and more in control.

Motivation Barrier #10: Boredom

Many girls have told me that sheer boredom is the one thing that stands in their way of staying motivated to lose weight and become healthier.

They get tired of eating the same food, and grinding through the same exercises every day. They want variety and change!

Breaking the Barrier

This one is a simple—boredom is only a problem when you are on a strict diet, restricting the variety of foods you eat, or doing exactly the same exercises day in and day out. If you follow all the guidelines in this book, you will feel satisfied, interested, and motivated!

Now you have all the tools you need—food knowledge, exercise skills, and motivation—to become the healthiest person you can be. I know you can do it, if you just take it one day at a time. With each small or big step forward, you can be really proud of yourself!

A Final Word

Knowledge Is Power

Congratulations! You did it—you read the whole book. That's a big accomplishment, because it means you've come a very long way toward having the knowledge you need to become healthier and happier. You may have heard the saying "knowledge is power." Well it's true—knowledge really is power. In this case, it's the power to recognize what you need to change in order to be healthy. It is also the power to look at yourself carefully and decide you are not going to continue a relationship with food that is bad for you physically and emotionally. Knowledge will also infuse you with the power to realize that neither food nor exercise is your enemy. Rather, now you have learned that positive relationships with both food and exercise are necessary for you to feel and look healthy.

Now you also have the power to cope with people in your life—family, friends, guys—in a way that will not include using food to manage your feelings. You have lots of tools to separate yourself from negative friendships and to focus on positive friendships. You have tools to communicate with your parents better in order to help them understand you. And you have tools to choose guys that respect and value you. Now that you have knowledge, you understand yourself much better too. You have the power to change unhealthy or self-destructive patterns. You also have the power to think about the role that food and exercise has (or hasn't) played in your life and begin to make healthy changes.

Last, but perhaps most important, the knowledge you've gathered from this book will give you the power to be the healthiest and happiest *you* possible! Now you know that you have me to help you. Remember, I've been where you're coming from, so I know you can get to where you want to be.

As you have seen, in order for *Dr. Susan's Girls-Only Weight Loss Guide* to help, you need to look closely at your eating and exercise habits. But as you have also figured out, it is just as important to examine the role of your emotions and relationships. You saw this in the chapters discussing feelings, self-esteem, patterns, families, and friends. Remember, the power doesn't come from a diet or from going to the gym every day. It comes from understanding yourself, learning how and why your body isn't as healthy as it can be, and then making the emotional and lifestyle changes that you've learned so you can become healthier.

But what if you've tried everything in the book and you're still very overweight? If you've made a true commitment, for several months, to understanding your food and body-related feelings, eating healthily and exercising, but you just don't see it working, you need to reach out for more help. As I've suggested throughout the book, when you're confused, discouraged, or upset you need to speak to your parents, your doctor, your school counselor, or another trusted adult. In unusual instances there are medical reasons that can cause you to become overweight or make it very difficult to lose weight. A medical evaluation is the only way to figure this out. There are medical specialists who can diagnose whether your body isn't working properly to keep your weight where it should be. If you are diagnosed with a medical condition that causes weight gain, these doctors will also help you and your parents decide what medical treatment will best benefit your body and lifestyle.

But, remember, *a medical reason for being overweight is, by far, the exception*. Some girls wish they could be "cured" by medication or surgery, or at least have a good reason for why they've gained so much weight. The reality is that in almost all cases, you will be able to become significantly healthier and look much better if you closely follow *Dr. Susan's Girls-Only Weight Loss Guide.*

So, take control of your life! Take responsibility for how you look and feel. I'm right there with you and I know that you can do it. Along your journey, I'd love to hear how you're doing. So email me at DrSusan@girlsonlyweightloss.com.

Meet the Girls Advisory Group

As I have discussed throughout *Dr. Susan's Girls-Only Weight Loss Guide* I had a truly incredible group of twelve girls, each who contributed uniquely to this book. Now it's time for you to meet them. Each girl tells her own story in order to share a bit about herself with you. I'm sure you will recognize yourself in some of these descriptions and I hope you will enjoy reading about these strong, intelligent, and wonderful girls. If you would like to contact any of the girls you can do so by emailing me at DrSusan@girlsonlyweightloss.com.

My name is Alexis Bevilacqua. I am sixteen years old and I am a high school junior (11th grade). Body image has been a major problem for me ever since I hit thirteen. I started to look at magazines and wanted to look just like the models. I wanted to change so much about my body but I realized there was only one thing I could change myself—my weight. I have a hard time admitting that I am overweight. I have had many struggles in trying to lose weight. Food is basically everywhere you go, so there are always opportunities to overeat. Another struggle has been differentiating when I am hungry from when I am bored. Working on this book, I met a lot of great girls who shared similar problems. I think that with the advice from Dr. Susan and my peers, I'll be able to reach a healthy weight. I would advise girls reading this book that your family is important and if you feel you don't have their support you need to talk to them and say "listen, I'm going to do this and I need you to support me." Explain your goals and tell them you're doing this for yourself and you want them to respect this.

My name is Montserrat Del Olmo and I'm a sixteen-year-old Hispanic girl who came to the United States at age five. Being the only girl in the family, I was never really worried about my body because I play many sports with my two brothers. My brothers are more carefree about their bodies and are a great influence on me and how I look at my body. Although I've never had weight problems, I have many friends that do. Seeing the problems in others, I try hard to understand what goes through their minds. I know that the media is wrong to make skinny women seem beautiful and I deeply believe that nonanorexic women are beautiful. It is my belief that most men prefer women with curves than those without. Respecting everyone's right to like different body types, I believe that as long as you aren't either of the extremes (obese or anorexic) you can live a healthy and happy life. Being in the group gave me an even clearer perspective from the heavier girls and helped me understand where they're coming from. The group also gave me a sense of utmost respect for girls who try to change their ways to have a healthier body.

Hi! My name is Chantal Dumpson. I am a very athletic person and in pretty good shape. But I believe that there is so much more I can learn about living a healthy lifestyle. I was excited when I began working on the book and it was an incredible experience. I met new people and gained insight into some things I've never really thought about before. During those months, I've learned about the risks of unhealthy eating habits and about eating disorders. I think you'll learn a lot from *Dr. Susan's Girls-Only Weight Loss Guide* because it contains the input of girls from different backgrounds and lifestyles. Also, looking into the way you eat and exercise helps you learn new things about yourself. I strongly recommend this book to EVERY teenage girl. Thanks for reading it!

My name is Jessica Dumpson and I am fifteen years old. I have been working on this book with the rest of the group for a long time and I have really enjoyed it. I liked meeting new people and the group helped me a lot, both physically and emotionally. It helped me learn how to eat in a healthier way, and it helped me to feel better about myself. I have a lot more confidence in myself now. I think it is very important for all girls to have a high level of self-esteem and confidence. I truly believe that this book helps a great deal. It will leave you feeling really, truly beautiful.

Hey, here's a little about myself. I'm Eve Eichenholtz. I am an 18-year-old heading off to college. I spend my time doing stage crew for theater productions, volunteering, teaching, and participating in many different clubs. In my busy schedule, exercise tends to be one of the first things to fall out. Despite the lack of time that I take to care for myself I am still happy with who I am. I tend to be confident, happy, and out-going and let very little stand in my way. Basically who I am is me, and whoever that is, is fine by me. Being part of this book was an enjoyable experience, and also one during which my knowledge about myself grew. I hope that as you use *Dr. Susan's Girls-Only Weight Loss Guide* it will help you to grow and become a healthier and happier you.

My name is Anna Evans and I am fifteen years old. I grew up in the Midwest with both my parents and two sisters (one older and one younger). We moved to the East Coast when I was in seventh grade because my mom got a new job. My hobbies are hanging out with friends, dancing, working out, being online and on the phone, and fashion. I am not satisfied with my body, but I like doing good things for myself (eating right, exercising properly, and doing things that make me happy). One of the many things I have learned about health and fitness is that you can't fool yourself by "going on a diet." In order to change your body, you have to really want to do it. Some people may think "I want to but I just can't lose the weight" (or whatever you want to change), but I am telling you that is not impossible. So believe in yourself and good luck to all of you. Enjoy this book. Dr. Susan knows what she's talking about!

My name is Jaime Feather and I am seventeen years old and a high school senior. I have had a weight problem ever since I can remember. Throughout my elementary and some of my middle school years, I was teased because of my weight. As I became a preteen and teen I began to realize that I also made myself feel uncomfortable around my peers because of my weight. I became more aware of what I could do to improve not only the way I looked, but the way I felt, (as *Dr. Susan's Girls-Only Weight Loss Guide* will teach you). I have come to discover that drinking at least six to eight glasses of water a day, plenty of exercise, and a healthy diet has helped me lose weight. Helping with this book was a great experience. While getting to know a group of girls who have experienced many of the same things as me, I also learned more about myself, both physically and emotionally. After you finish reading this book, I think you will discover it is one of the most informative and interesting books for girls. You must have the motivation to improve your health before you can take the steps to do so. One last thing: losing weight is not easy, but it isn't impossible either.

My name is Katherine Hartman. I have been overweight all my life. Combined with my height (5'9") I have run into many problems when my friends and I go shopping because most of them can wear normal, juniors' clothing, and I can't. Just this year I had my junior prom and finding a dress was a real nightmare. I did eventually find a dress I loved, but it was just another reminder that I need to lose weight. I love the theater and participate any way I can. But I think being overweight makes it harder for me to get parts in plays because the skinny, graceful girl is more likely to get the role than the heavy one. The fact that my older brother eats everything in sight and still looks like a toothpick doesn't make life any easier. I try to diet, but nothing works. I hope that I will eventually lose weight so my friends and I can shop in the same departments. Taking part in the group to help with this book really helped me realize that other people suffer from this as much as I do. This book will help girls deal with the same issues that we deal with.

My name is Michelle Guidice and I have two younger sisters and a younger brother. I'm seventeen years old and I've been on the varsity bowling team for three years. Once of my favorite activities is watching baseball. I love to go to the stadium with my family. I also like to watch auto racing. I have played soccer and softball since elementary school. It's been a lot of fun being in this group and I'm enjoyed discussing the chapters with Dr. Susan and the other girls.

My name is Michal Lucas and I am fifteen years old. I have been helping to write this book to encourage teenage girls to feel good about their bodies. Personally, I am happy with my body and feel that my personality and characteristics are more important than my appearance. While writing this book, I realized that it was helpful to talk to peers about the problems they faced. It showed me that others are experiencing the same feelings and have similar thoughts to me. I have learned that expressing one's feelings in a group can help a person through the problems they are facing. You should work hard to feel great about yourself, but you should also be satisfied with who you are as a person. I hope you enjoy the book and that it helps you with the challenges you might face in the future.

Hi, my name is **Burgandy McCurty**. I'm fourteen and going into ninth grade. I like to do math and science. I participate in soccer, volleyball, basketball, and lacrosse. It is very important to me to be active. I had a great experience working on *Dr. Susan's Girls-Only Weight Loss Guide* because I loved hearing the different opinions on body image. Everybody is different, some things come easier to some people and some things don't. It would be great if the girls reading this book could realize that it isn't about the TV, movie, and magazine images—you can learn to be happy with yourself.

My name is **Kelly Woolf** and I have struggled with my weight all my life. I know that the more you want to change the harder it gets! This struggle might be the hardest of my life and I know of many others. I have tried many diets; I have gone to weight loss camp, and all my life I have been trying to keep it under control. IT'S HARD! There are so many girls with eating disorders and weight-related diseases that the most important lesson I have learned is to lose weight healthily. Although I sometimes get off the "good track" with my weight, I know that it's not only important to how I look but for my health. My emotions have always affected my weight with the ups and downs of my life mirroring the ups and downs of my weight. I'm still learning how to handle my emotions and feelings without letting it affect my eating and weight. As I continue to try my hardest to overcome this obstacle, I advise you to do the best you can to be healthy. Losing weight will be a life long struggle for some and for others it will come easily, but just try. YOU'RE WORTH IT!

Contributors

Jamie Bliss, M.S.W.

Jamie is a clinical social worker who specializes in the treatment of eating disorders. She received her Masters Degree in 2000 from Adelphi University. Jamie is an associate of Dr. Ira Sacker, and has offices in Brooklyn and Long Island, New York. Jamie is a noted public speaker, who has made several television appearances, and has lectured at many schools and community groups. Jamie's approach to treating patients is quite unique, as she herself suffered with anorexia since the age of fifteen. She has found that patients appreciate the fact that she truly knows where they are coming from. She is able to provide living proof to her patients that it is possible to recover from an eating disorder.

Bev Francis

Bev contributed her awesome knowledge for the exercise chapter. She has a university degree in Physical Education from the University of Melbourne, Australia, and a Diploma of Teaching. She was a high school physical education and math teacher for eight years. Bev was on the

Australian Track and Field team for five years during which she broke the Australian shotput record (cool huh!). Then, she became the World Powerlifting (a kind of weight lifting) Champion, broke more than forty world powerlifting records and is still undefeated (wow!). She was the first woman to bench press more than 300 pounds. Bev was the star of the movie *Pumping Iron II: The Women* (1985) and is also the coauthor of *Bev Francis' Powerbodybuilding Book*. Bev and her husband Steve Weinberger own Bev Francis Powerhouse Gym in Syosset, New York. She also wants you to know that she is the mother of two girls.

Bonnie Heyman

Bonnie contributed tons of time and information to the exercise chapter. She has a B.A. in Dance from Adelphi University. She has also been a certified personal trainer for over 15 years and believes that with hard work anyone can achieve her fitness goals. Bonnie was a competitive body builder from 1991 to 1995 and she has a bunch of trophies to prove it. She is a certified Power Pilates instructor and teaches Power Pilates to children, teens and adults. Bonnie is a strength and endurance coach for a girls' gymnastics team. She also teaches the girls about healthy eating for gymnastics and for life.

Reed Mangels, Ph.D., R.D.

Dr. Reed Mangels contributed all the information about healthy vegetarian eating. She is a Nutrition Advisor for the nonprofit, educational Vegetarian Resource Group as well as nutrition editor and a regular columnist for the *Vegetarian Journal,* which is published four times a year. She is the coauthor of *Simply Vegan* and *Vegetarian FAQ.*

Judy Marshel, Ph.D., R.D., CD-N

Dr. Judy Marshel contributed a huge amount of nutritional information, as well as lots of facts about eating disorders. She also read and edited the whole manuscript. Dr. Marshel is an awesome and giving person. For 14 years she was the senior nutritionist for Weight Watchers International. Now Dr. Marshel has her own health-consulting practice (in Smithtown, Great Neck, and Brooklyn, NY) helping people (including many teenage girls) have healthier lives. She has also written two books, *Trouble-Free Menopause* and *PMS Relief.*

Ira M. Sacker, MD

Dr. Sacker provided me with tons of information about the development of pre-teen and teenage girls, as well as lots of knowledge about eating disorders. Until recently he was the Director of Adolescent and Young Adult Medicine at the Brookdale University Hospital and Medical Center in Brooklyn, NY. He is also the founder and director of HEED (Helping End Eating Disorders) Foundation, which is dedicated to the education, prevention, and treatment of eating disorders. Dr. Sacker is the author of an important book, *Dying to Be Thin*, which can teach you a lot about eating disorders.

Organizations, Websites, Books, and Other Useful Stuff

If You Think You (or Someone Else) May Have a Problem with Alcohol

→ Alcoholics Anonymous
www.Alcoholics-Anonymous.org
Look up "Alcoholics Anonymous" in your local telephone book

→ Al-Anon/Alateen
www.Al-Anon.org
www.alateen.org
1-888-4AL-ANON [1-888-425-2666]

Help with Depression, Suicidal Thoughts, and Other Bad Feelings

→ Focus Adolescent Services
www.focusas.com
1-877-362-8727

→ Childhelp USA
   www.childhelpusa.org/child/hotline
   1- 800-4-A-CHILD [1-800-422-4453]

→ Girls and Boys Town
   www.girlsandboystown.org
   1-800-448-3000

Learn More About Cigarettes, Drugs, Diet Pills, and Other Addictive Substances

→ About.com Smoking Cessation website
   http://www.quitsmoking.about.com/cs/teens

→ The Foundation for a Smokefree America
   www.NoTobacco.org

→ The National Clearinghouse for Alcohol and Drug Information
   www.health.org
   1-800-729-6686

Being a Vegetarian

→ Vegetarian Resource Group
   www.vrg.org
   Email: vrg@vrg.org
   P.O. Box 1463, Baltimore, MD 21203
   (410) 366-VEGE [410-366-8343]

Cooking Books

→ *Clueless in the Kitchen: A Cookbook for Teens* (Firefly)
   by Evelyn Raab

→ *A Teen's Guide to Going Vegetarian* (Puffin) by Judy Krizmanic

→ *The Teen's Vegetarian Cookbook* (Viking Press) by Judy Krizmanic

→ *Vegetables Rock! A Complete Guide for Teenage Vegetarians* (Bantam Books) by Stephanie Pierson

Help with Eating Disorders

→ Anorexia Nervosa and Related Eating Disorders, Inc. (ANRED)
www.anred.com
Email: jarinor@rio.com
(541) 344-1144

→ National Association of Anorexia Nervosa and Associated Disorders (ANAD)
www.anad.org
Email: ANAD20@aol.com
(847) 831-3438

→ Overeaters Anonymous
www.oa.org
info@oa.org
(505) 891-2664

→ The HEED Foundation (Helping End Eating Disorders)
www.heedfoundation.org
helpline@heedfoundation.org
(516) 694-1054

Index